The Christian Atheist

Integrating Science, Psychology, Medicine and Spirituality in the 21st Century

By

Robert R. Blake, Ph.D.

This book is a work of fiction. Places, events, and situations in this story are purely fictional. Any resemblance to actual persons, living or dead, is coincidental.

ISBN: 1-4033-3263-0 (e-book)
ISBN: 1-4033-3264-9 (Paperback)
ISBN: 1-4033-3265-7 (Hardcover)

Library of Congress Control Number: 2002092088

This book is printed on acid free paper.

Printed in the United States of America
Bloomington, IN

1stBooks - rev. 12/10/02

Dedication

To Logan, Chelsea, and Shannon who, like all of us, must come to their own conclusion.

Chapter Titles

Bringing Spirituality Up to Date

Science without religions is lame,
Religion without science is blind.
(Albert Einstein)

Until I went to seminary to become a minister, God and I were very close. Then I got "educated" and God died. For many years I have been a very comfortable Christian Atheist. But just as my former childlike beliefs about God conflicted with science and had to be abandoned, so too did my intellectual atheism eventually prove too sterile for the continuing wonders that both science and life reveal.

So what is a person to do who isn't comfortable with a "take it on faith" or "the Bible says so" approach to spirituality, but in their heart they believe in something important beyond themselves? Some go into a Sunday morning intellectual trance or brain lock and accept some form of mythical theology that conflicts with everything else they know about how the world operates. Some push spiritual issues to the very vague background and declare: "I believe, but I don't go to church or pray or anything." Some, however, want to remain intellectually and scientifically rigorous and yet figure out how spirituality can still be an honest part of our lives. That is the task of this book.

For the twenty-first century we need a spiritual understanding that is compatible with science, logic, and every day experience. If not, it is irrelevant to our everyday life and is left to some separate, smaller portion of our lives that only applies to quiet meditative moments, religious services, and when we have really big problems. All and all, those are just a few moments out of our lives. If religion and spirituality are going to have any real significance, it has to have something to do with our everyday lives and yet fit in with modern scientific understandings of the universe. The laws of nature and science cannot be put on "Pause" like a rental movie when we start dealing with spiritual understanding.

Discovery, invention, creativity, and change happen faster and faster every day. We should also expect that our spiritual understanding will also change and evolve. Just as the information required to build computers existed 2,000 and 10 billion years ago, but was not yet discovered and understood, we should not assume that everything there is to understand about spirituality was discovered a long time ago and will never expand. Historically based religions have important values to teach and have the ability to nurture our spiritual nature, but those teachings need to evolve beyond the outdated mythologies and world-views in which they originated. We can't expect our prophets to be riding donkeys anymore. There is plenty to excite us, astound us, and humble us in the 21st century. Life doesn't stay the same as in the first or any other century. Life and knowledge evolve. Religious faith and understanding must evolve too. The religious teachings, scriptures, and traditions of the centuries still contain many meaningful and uplifting insights, but they also contain references and assumptions that we no longer find useful, accurate, or believable. Spiritual experiences and appreciation for the holiness of life do not disappear if we give up old ways of thinking and believing. In fact religious faith, just like life itself, can only survive if it changes and evolves. Spiritual insight does not have to rest on believing things that are totally at odds with everything else we know—like the universe being created in seven days or an executed man's body getting up and walking around. These same amazing feelings of wonder, appreciation, and inspiration to which these myths point can emerge from our own experience of life, in our own time, and within our own current knowledge and experiences of the world.

Organized religions have often encouraged faith without proof. Science has often encouraged proof without faith. Both of these approaches understate the totality of our human existence. Science is not a matter of what is "out there in the objective world" and faith a matter of what is "in here in our subjective hopes and needs". Psychology, religion, and science are coming back together to create new forms of spiritual and theological understanding. Both our internal experience and feelings and our external objective knowledge are necessary to create spiritual understanding today. Without integrating our knowledge of human consciousness and emotion into our understanding of reality, we have only intellectualized materialism and determinism. Without scientific knowledge and intellectual consistency we have only our fears, feelings, and fantasies upon which to build a spiritual framework.

Religious faith is often presented like a rock in a stream, the Rock of Salvation. Grab onto the rock or you will be swept away! Stay grounded here where it is safe! But life is an ever-flowing stream and it already has gone by a lot of those old rocks that seemed safe to stand on. Knowledge and history has moved on, and we with it. If we are to have a spiritual understanding or religious faith to handle the life-currents that we are now encountering, we better have a spirituality that has taught us to swim and adjust to the currents rather than hang onto old certainties that are long ago passed by. Ironically, the best way to have a vibrant spirituality is not to cling onto ideas from the past, but to let go of them and let our spirituality evolve from our encounter with life now. Then we can judge how our current experience matches up against the spiritual experience and insight of our ancestors. That which is true and important from past belief systems will find a place in its own way along side our current understanding of the way the world is. It is more intellectually honest, and ultimately builds more vibrant spirituality, to let any truths from historical based religions to emerge from our current knowledge than to twist our current understanding to fit ancient world-views.

We still will ask the same questions: Where did we come from? Why are we here? Does anyone care about us? Why do bad things happen? Our desire for answers to difficult soul-searching questions does not justify suspending current levels of knowledge, logic, and experience to embrace impossibly antiquated religious and theological explanations. Because we want reassuring answers, we sometimes are tempted to accept the most bizarre explanations, dubious sources, and inexplicable logic, totally contradictory to everything else science has shown us; but this is not necessary. We can incorporate our current knowledge base and still be spiritual. If there is a God, it must be a unifying concept that ties everything together, not one that causes logic and experience to be suspended and encourages acceptance of miracles, magic, and lower levels of proof than we would require from our local auto mechanic.

"Show me how that works. How do you know that's true? How can you prove that? What evidence is there to support what you are saying?" Well founded, intelligent skepticism is healthy in spiritual matters just as it is in claims for a better carpet sweeper or life on Mars. Curiosity coupled with intellectual honesty, even if it is unsettling sometimes, will always lead to more thoughtful living as well as increased spiritual understanding. It has not proven effective to take things "on faith" without logic or proof in other parts of our lives. Why should we act any differently in areas of spirituality? Why should we base something as important as our spiritual beliefs on things that can't be proved or that are unknown?

If the plumber says I need a new septic system, I want to know why. I want another opinion, and I certainly trust my own logic. I want to understand why. My wife hates my questioning. She wisely won't talk to any of the service people and relay messages back to me because I always ask her "Why is that?" or "That doesn't make any sense because…" Sometimes she feels I'm questioning the accuracy of her reporting or her logic and takes it personally. So if we're going to take the time to question the plumber when our basement stinks of sewage and needs to be fixed immediately, and even run the risk that our questioning will get us cross-wise with our spouse (which together can make for a very stinko week), why wouldn't we question spiritual and theological explanations just as carefully?

Not only am I sympathetic to "Doubting Thomas" in the New Testament gospel stories who wanted to see the nail holes in the hands of what was supposed to be a Jesus risen from the dead after being nailed to a cross to die. I also want the blood tested to make sure it's not ketchup and a DNA study to see if it is really the same guy. Why would we easily accept an unlikely story about dead people getting up and walking around unless we were also going to accept tabloid claims of our abducted neighbors having children with space aliens? Most of us don't believe tabloid sensationalism at the supermarket check-out lane. Why should we act any differently about our spiritual and religious beliefs? When we are young or new in our understanding of spiritual issues, miraculous stories and less rigorously examined statements of faith are quite eye catching—kind of like the hardware store giving away a new lawn mower in order to attract more customers. But splashy advertising, something for nothing, and miraculous luck is not the core business for hardware stores nor should it be for our spiritual business. As we grow in our understanding and experience, we go to the hardware store to get the things we really need anyway, not really expecting to win the lawn mower. Our spiritual beliefs needs to be similar: quite sufficient to support our everyday needs, lifting our spirits, but not needing miracles and unlikely promises to influence our decision making.

We can have the same sense of awe and majesty today that ancient nomads had when they gazed at the stars and wondered which god had shaken the dust from their sandals upon the blackness of the sky. In fact we can be even more in awe because we know that the shining of the stars we are observing are light years away—that is light traveling at 186,000 miles per second—still taking millions of years to reach us—so far away that the star we see may have burned out and not exist anymore by the time we see it. Wow! Wow! Woooooooow! Now that really is amazing and awe-inspiring! Is that any less majestic and humbling than what our nomadic ancestors believed? The purpose of this book is to be reverential and amazed by what we understand and experience, not by what we do not know and could not happen. It is an attempt to understand spirituality with the knowledge we now have in science, psychology, medicine, and human consciousness.

Whom Can You Trust About What to Believe?

We should look at New Age Religion
Just as reverently and skeptically
As we look at Old Age Religion.
Inspiration usually comes
When we're not certain.

Even as children we have the unspoken understanding that spiritual teachings and religious stories really aren't like real life. We were supposed to get the moral to the story without really believing the story—like the story of Jesus praying over a few fish and loaves of bread and then all the hundreds of people who were gathered supposedly eating these meager morsels and feeling full. They were full of something, but it probably wasn't bread and fish. Maybe they were filled with love, or their hearts were filled with the emotion of sharing whatever they had. Because these stories were, and often still are, presented as factual (except in those new bibles where they take unlimited liberties in reinterpreting what was originally written), it is difficult for a child, let alone an adult, to think religious teachings are based on facts. A good science fiction fantasy such as the movie story of the friendly space alien E.T. can entertain and even inspire us just like the stories that convey religious teachings, but we know they couldn't possibly happen in the world in which we really live. In the mistaken belief that unchanging stories and historical traditions have more authority or depth of authenticity, many religions have felt obligated to maintain stories and explanations that are non-science fiction.

Being a preacher's kid gave me an advantage in sorting out the "real" religious stuff from the fantasy. We were poor. We were also happy, but not able to afford luxuries such as Welch's grape juice in our house. But when Communion Sunday rolled around about 4 times a year, the reward for spending a couple of hours on Saturday evening cutting up an entire loaf of bread into little cubes for the communion service that were so small you could barely taste them, was that you got to sneak down a couple of little communion cups of grape juice. (Methodists weren't allowed to drink grown up wine back then. In fact when we traveled, my father would go into the restaurants to see if they served alcohol while the rest of the family hid anxiously in the car to see if it was safe, or whether we'd have to go starving on down the road to find another place to eat.) To me, that grape juice was very, very <u>fine</u>! Right up there with drinking the maraschino cherry juice straight out of the jar. Of course, if we didn't have a big crowd at church, I got to dispose of all the leftovers too. Those little cups were only about a quarter the size of a shot glass, but you could get to feeling real good if you downed 20 or 30 of those little suckers.

Now with that kind of experience before and after "Holy Communion", you can see it was pretty easy not to take the ceremony literally, but to try to understand the symbolism. My father, following the prescribed ritual in the impressively bound black leather book, lifted the cup and read:

> He took the cup; and when He had given thanks, He gave it to them saying, Drink ye all of this; for this is My blood of the new Testament, which is shed for you and for many, for the remission of sins; do this, as oft as ye shall drink it, in remembrance of Me. (The Methodist Hymnal, 1939.)

I knew this had to be symbolic, because I myself poured the grape juice in there, and did a little experiment (all in the name of science, of course) by tasting it before and after it was blessed. I can tell you for sure, it wasn't blood; it was Welch's. Unmistakable difference there! Kids don't mix those two up every easily. Apparently confusion about religious symbolism is left to adults.

Being Right

Church teachings often treat historical religious metaphors and symbols similar to Santa Claus. Even after you know the truth, you aren't supposed to tell anyone for fear you'll ruin the good times for the next generation of kids/membership class. Eventually people stop believing in Santa Claus but instead emphasize the spirit of Christmas. Historically based religions tend to be limited in theological concepts for grown ups, offer little to help replace or even reinterpret the ancient myths and metaphors, and do not have a theological framework to incorporate new modern discoveries that transcend ancient religious teachings and texts. Adults are still asked to get up in front of a congregation of peers and profess belief in childlike magical concepts which they outgrew with Santa Claus in order to become members of a faith community. What are we to do if we want all the values of ancient religious teachings but in a grown-up version? It is not necessary to sort through or ignore ancient mythology, unacceptable priestly pronouncements, and outdated concepts to celebrate the values addressed in these teachings.

1400 years ago a merchant in the Middle East began articulating a new spiritual faith that, like its Judeo-Christian counterpart, emphasized one powerful god. These teachings were also claimed to come directly from God, referred to as Allah, and were eventually collected into one book, the Koran. Just as early Judaism became more institutionalized beyond its early prophets, later priests and writers extended both religious traditions into rules to live by. As in most religions, a portion of this belief system evolved which emphasized following their rules to show one's faithfulness, but things change. It seems unlikely that a rule to avoid eating pork would evolve the same way in a society that has refrigeration, controlled cooking, and meat thermometers than when these rules were formulated in early Jewish history. Perhaps the rules about women wearing veils would evolve differently in current Islamic culture where it is no longer the custom for women to go about with the upper half of their body uncovered as it was in the time of Mohammed. We don't execute criminals by crucifixion any more, so modern symbols for Christianity would likely take another form than a cross. Things change.

Our current spirituality cannot rest on things that were once revealed or are unknown but stems inevitably from our own current experience, reason, and emotional sensitivities. We listen to all the wisdom of our ancestors, sift it through our own experience, listen to the beliefs of others, and then choose what we will believe and how we will live. It is not necessary for Born again Christians to stop quoting the Bible or believing in Heaven and Hell nor that some of the rest of us have to start. It just requires recognizing that we're all doing our best to figure this life thing out and deserve mutual respect for seeking to live our lives with moral discernment. Let us stop praying (or worse actions) that the "non-believers" will be converted to our point of view. Perhaps it is more helpful to humbly share how difficult it is to keep our own lives running straight, with all of our own mistakes, than it is to proclaim that we know how someone else should run his or her life.

I always enjoyed the story of St. Peter showing a new arrival around heaven:

> "Over here are the Methodists. Over there by the pagoda, of course, are the Taoists, Confucianists, and ancestor worshippers. Over here you will find the Buddhists and the Baptists and the Jews"
>
> Suddenly they came to a tall brick wall that stretched off in both directions. The new visitor asked: "That's strange to see a wall up here where everyone seems equally accepted. What's it doing here?"

> "Shhhhh", said St. Peter.
> "The Fundamentalists are over there. We don't like to bother them. They like to think they're the only ones here."

When we don't have any hope of perceiving all of the complexities of the universe, and we have only our human intelligence and senses to conceptualize it, for any of us to claim we have the only version of the Truth only reveals the limitation of our spiritual enlightenment. It is comforting to believe that our own religious texts, our own priests, or own philosophical understandings are absolutely true, but we'll have to settle only for hoping that our version of the truth will help us make meaning for our own lives and not harm others. It is a bit unsettling and uncomfortable trying to understand and proclaim the purpose of our entire existence by things that are limited by our own understanding and which we know will be superseded by future understandings and enlightenment.

There were so many people debating about accounts of the life of Jesus and other religious texts vying for official recognition that the early church conference delegates had to vote on their favorites. They voted to include four different accounts of Jesus' life, one each by Matthew, Mark, Luke, and John. There is always a lot of behind the scenes politicking and maneuvering that goes into picking which books are going to be included in a bible, or which Cardinal is going to get chosen Pope, or which division head will succeed to the chairmanship of General Motors. Thoughtful deliberation produces the best decision possible in all theses cases, but to claim any of these as God's last word or only revelation ignores not only historical reality but also our own experience.

Sadly some of the most vicious acts in history have been performed in the name of insuring religious authority, purity and correctness.

> "The first English version of the Scriptures made by direct translation from the original Hebrew and Greek, and the first to be printed, was the work of William Tyndale. He met bitter opposition. He was accused of willfully perverting the meaning of the Scriptures, and his New Testaments were ordered to be burned as "untrue translations." He was finally betrayed into the hands of his enemies, and in October 1536, was publicly executed and burned at the stake." (Holy Bible. Revised Standard Version.)

Yet subsequent translations, including the King James Version, relied heavily on Tyndale's work. Even within the last fifty years similarly vigorous verbal attacks were directed at anyone who dared print a different translation than the off-spring of this formerly burned version of "The Word of God". It appears throughout history that whatever version of religious truth is currently ascribed to is often thought to be the only accurate one.

In the late 1960s I was an associate minister in a Methodist church in Evanston, Illinois, a suburb of Chicago. People who were dedicated to social justice, equal housing, and celebrating with new music and worship forms (balloons and banners were really big then) gathered at this church where I begged my way onto the staff. I was reading books in seminary studies entitled The Death of God and Situational Ethics, and discovering that no "new" theological idea is any more radical than what theologians from centuries earlier have quietly written on the same topic. In retrospect I have a lot more empathy, respect, and understanding for the older, long standing members of this church. They had a nice quiet place in which to worship in a traditional way, not having to deal with marching in the streets for equal education, housing, or opportunities, nor deal with conscientious objection to a war, nor unfamiliar sounding theology and new forms of worship, nor pool tables and rock bands in the basement for the kids. They wanted their church to be a comfortable place that supported and valued their beliefs and their traditional way of life. Somehow their church became over-run by an infestation of overly enthusiastic iconoclasts who challenged their thoughts and changed their ways of worship. The more traditional members felt they were losing their church, the spiritual traditions in which they found comfort, and the expression of spiritual celebration with which they were familiar.

I left that church and organized religion and the senior pastor moved on to another church. I left primarily because it felt tiring and somewhat dishonest, to keep translating into God language, my more secular understanding of spiritual matters. I knew my upbringing in the Church was really important to me. It left me believing that all people are created equal and deserve to be treated with respect, from bishops to lepers, bank presidents to laborers, all both saints and sinners equally. I learned that being loving toward others and allowing others to love us is perhaps the most important thing. These are values and principles of living that I verified in my own experience. Live up to the highest standards you embrace, and forgive yourself when you occasionally fall short. This remained a really good philosophy to live by, even after I discarded the theological explanation from which I first learned it: that we sinners are acceptable to God only because Christ died for our sins. That explanation lost meaning and therefore importance, but experience verified these were good principles and worked well in life. Because I had the belief and commitment but couldn't accept explanations at odds with modern knowledge and rational thought, I decided I'd probably set my path outside organized religion.

As soul-searching, invigorating, and frightening as that and other personal decisions were, it was the aftershock that left that most long lasting impression. Shortly after the senior pastor and I left this local church, the Democratic National Convention was held in Chicago. This was a time of large protests and, some say, police riots. The Students for a Democratic Society (SDS) were one of those protesting groups. They were a somewhat motley bunch of young people who wanted to be heard, and who were somewhat undisciplined in both their seriousness and their fun. They found a place to sleep during their stay in Chicago. That place, of course, was in the basement of the church next to the pool table. In retrospect maybe the church should not have provided them shelter. Some of their protesting behavior down in Grant Park was often disrespectful, obnoxious, illegal, or perhaps worse; but what happened next kept me away from any church for 25 years. Some of the old-faithful church members, who understandably had felt displaced and threatened by all these changes, were now emboldened with the departure of the new breed of ministers. So they reclaimed their church by gathering to beat up these young people and drive them from their church. Fists and baseball bats in the name of God!

Though I was probably headed in that direction anyway, this expression of Christian fervor convinced me to abandon organized religion. I wanted them to have their church back! I wanted to associate with people who weren't so sure they were right, with people who feel that honest questioning is as spiritually important as religious certainty, believing that listening to more points of view brings more wisdom than vehemently proclaiming our own truth. I became convinced that as spiritual believers become more certain that they are uniquely right, they only become closer to being completely wrong.

The Ultimate Authority on Spiritual Matters

Religious tradition, practices, and scriptures are sources of inspiration to some people, but are often disconnected from the everyday life of American society. There are certainly some good stories, poetry, and inspirational thoughts in these written collections of the many different oral traditions that were passed on and edited from one generation to the next, but ancient religious texts are somewhat like my computer instructions. Some chapters are just written poorly or hard to understand. Some of it I'll never use and just ignore. Some of the applications do not apply to things I'm doing. I love the word processing but the plastic wrap is still on the financial spread sheet instructions and I'll probably never open them before I get another computer which will have a later and better version. The Bible and other religious writings are the same way. Some of the poetry of the Psalms is beautiful, but Revelations reminds me of scribblings people used to hand me on the mental hospital ward; and I really don't personally expect to have much use for the lengthy account of the family lineage of Esau; and there have been more than a few discoveries about the origins of the universe since the account in the book of Genesis. Most people just ignore or dismiss some parts of both religious and secular manuals which they don't understand or don't seem to apply. It's normal to expect that sometimes we'll find later versions or new explanations that are more helpful and useful, but organized religions have resisted this evolution.

For instance, in the biblical story of Moses it is scientifically highly unlikely that a one-time unique act of nature caused the Red Sea to temporarily split in half so Moses could lead his people to freedom from slavery in Egypt. It is much more likely that during the dry season the marsh land dried up enough to walk across it. Then the rains came and the land was covered with water again before Pharaoh could get his army together to recapture and enslave the Jews. That is a more likely analytical and scientifically plausible explanation. But to express the joy of being freed from slavery is better expressed in joyous song, prayers of thanksgiving, and proclamations of miracles than it is in explanations of a rainless Spring and good luck. To embrace the full meaning of an event, we must integrate our reasoned and logical thinking with our emotional and spiritual feelings; but the views must complement, not oppose, each other. To use science and logic to explain our human experience without including human emotion is just as incomplete as trusting human emotion and fantasy to shape our spiritual concepts without science and logic.

So to whom should we listen about spiritual understanding? Some years ago when I regularly used to go to O'Hare International Airport, visitors were always greeted at the main entrances by Hari Krishnas who were raising money. At first they chanted and had a cloth on the floor onto which people were encouraged to toss some coins. Then over the course of a year or two, they stopped ringing the cymbals and bells and simply had containers into which people were encouraged to slip some lose change or preferably bills. Then, as more public exasperation was voiced, some pretty bad looking wigs covered these shaved heads. The robes disappeared as well. Then, visitors were approached with a friendly, "Welcome to Chicago" and the offer of one of their free books—for a donation. Finally, the airport authority found a way to stop all soliciting, or the group just lost its karma, and they disappeared. Their religious pronouncements were suspect because they hustled everyone for money, not because their teachings were totally without merit. Some spiritual teachings will be rejected because they conflict with our experience or knowledge. Some will be rejected because we don't trust the messenger. Some will be rejected because they don't touch our spirit.

Martin Luther King's "I Have a Dream" speech at the March on Washington will always bring tears to my eyes. Are those words any less the words of God or less inspired than those of the Torah, Koran, or Bible? Ray Charles' rendition of America the Beautiful will always stir my heart more than those ponderous Germanic church hymns I grew up on. Sometimes we can be uplifted by the songs of the psalmists. Sometimes current lyricists better address our spirit. Inspiration and wisdom are all around us in both old and new forms and one form will not bring the same enlightenment to everyone.

So there is no one source for spiritual enlightenment or inspiration, but there is only one decisive authority on spiritual matters. In fact there cannot be any other authority on spiritual matters than ourselves. We always rely on our own judgment and decision making even when we pretend to give it to someone else. People memorize, underline, and repeat passages from religious and secular sources that they agree with or find inspiring. We ignore or discard the rest of it. We repeat religious teachings that we like or agree with and discard the others. The problem with admitting that we really are our own ultimate authority on moral and spiritual matters is that we have to admit there is no way to know for sure whether we're right. We might be wrong about the ultimate things, but that's always been true. Just because we bound the words in scrolls and leather binders and spoke them while wearing robes and hats does not mean they can't be wrong. If we are going to seek the Truth, we have to start by being honest.

Whether we embrace it or try to hide from it, we are the final authority on spiritual matters and what is right and meaningful in our own lives. We can accept or adopt other's thoughts, ideas, and expressions of faith or religion, but only we are allowed to write in our own book of spiritual insight and meaning. Our book may remain blank. It may have so many erasures in it that it is difficult to read. It can have only a few simple lines or phrases like "love your neighbor as you love yourself". In the end we cannot escape that we write our own spiritual bible. It is a humbling and somewhat frightening responsibility. But the person of faith says:

> I will live the best I can, to the highest I know, and believe in my heart that it is good enough; acceptable to whatever portion of the Universe that may notice. Having this amazing opportunity to proclaim the meaning of my own existence, I will accept it, embrace it, rejoice in it, and make the Universe better by one.

Myths and Other Sacred Packaging

There is a longing in our hearts, O Lord
For you to reveal yourself to us.
(Anne Quigley. From the Hymnal
of the Catholic Church)

The Santa Myth

Myths are stories or beliefs that we do not subject to our usual factual standards of truth because they convey another underlying truth or concept. The myth of Santa Claus is a wonderful way to convey a sense of universal love to children. Just because there isn't a real person called Santa Claus with a long white beard doesn't mean that sharing this myth with children is bad. It has a sense of wonder that fits our dreams and hopes. It conveys a sense of love, caring, and joy that both children and adults cherish. Eventually, of course, children come to realize that the bearded Santa Claus can't be real. Usually adults are more concerned about the disappointment this revelation may cause than it is traumatic for growing minds that are naturally expanding their knowledge of the world anyway. Adult forms of love, caring and joy are pretty wonderful too! Children eventually come to see that Santa Claus represents a spirit in all of us, and the love and joy in our own hearts is what makes the celebration of Santa Claus real for us.

Now try rereading the above paragraph substituting the word God for Santa Claus.

It is curious that many people do not worry that expressions of love, care, and joy will cease if we admit that the Santa Claus story is a myth we use to convey an underlying truth. Yet the same people can fear that our reverence, spirituality, and ethical behavior will stop if we admit that we use religious myths to convey underlying values. Children who no longer believe in Santa Claus do not cease to get love nor be loving, nor do people who do not believe in a human-like God suddenly stop getting love and acting in loving ways. Adults, more than children, struggle with the idea that many revered religious stories are myths. Kids are accustomed to making up stories and using fantasy, and when they want to know whether something really happened or not, they aren't afraid to ask. To admit that a cosmic father/mother like figure probably didn't create everything doesn't change the wonder, awe, and humbleness we feel when we contemplate how we got here and our place in the universe.

The reason many adults in American main stream religions seem to feel more comfortable retaining myths to explain their spirituality is because they haven't been given any alternative. More sophisticated options for conceptualizing or expressing spiritual concepts are seldom encouraged nor made available by organized religion. In the desire to support and explain spirituality, organized religions have offered traditional mythological explanations as facts. Stories and explanations from thousands of years ago, when there wasn't any scientific understanding, are presented as the basis upon which we should embrace spirituality in our lives today. This is like deciding to build a pyramid today, but saying you still have to move all the stone blocks by hand. Why would anyone want to try to do that? The invention of the wheel, understanding the nature of our solar system, and the development of fast food restaurants have all shaped our culture and how we live. The invention of the printing press, the Internet, millions more books from inspired hearts, and sending space probes to the outer reaches of the universe have not similarly shaped our theological and religious teachings.

There is usually little harm done in having childlike mythological concepts for cosmological explanations. But the neglect to integrate current knowledge into religious and cosmologial views tends to drive many thoughtful people away from churches and limit the influence of organized religions in our society primarily to passionate fundamentalists. Those who embrace traditional religious mythology are usually very good people. If everyone still believed in Santa Claus the quality of life and how we treat each other would not suffer. The same is true of spiritual mythology. It provides stories and vignettes that may inspire some people to center their lives in a reverential and helpful way. Some people, however, always want to know who is behind the Santa beard and wig and what is behind the religious mythology. "Inquiring minds want to know!" As Paul, the first century converted persecutor of Christians and later essentially the founder of the Christian church, said: "When I was a child, I spoke like a child, I thought like a child, I reasoned like a child; when I became an adult, I put an end to childish ways." (I Corinthians 13:11). It's time for us to explore a more adult understanding of spirituality.

Traditional Religious Mythology

The important part of a creation myth is not that a god made everything in 7 days or that P'an Ku was the first bigger than life size man who chiseled out places for valleys, and suns, separating heaven and earth and when he died and his remains formed the Five Sacred Mountains of China. We know this isn't factual. The important part of both these myths is that they address our deep feeling of wanting to belong, to know our place and purpose, and have some order and sense of direction in this otherwise pretty large and sometimes intimidating place we call the Universe. Myths are culture and time specific attempts to address our emotional needs and help guide our own behavior to be good and do good. The value for spiritual inspiration is diminished, however, if adults are asked to believe that reindeer really know how to fly, Jesus turned water into wine, and God created the universe in seven days. Any fourth grader can tell you that can't be true unless we deliberately withhold scientific facts from them.

Traditional religious values often still apply today. The reason to "honor you father and mother", however, is not because God sent a lightening bolt down, etched those words into solid stone tablets, and gave them to Moses. The reason to honor your father and mother is because we need people to love and support us while we grow up, our parents have more experience than we do, and they deserve our appreciation and respect for trying to help us. If children act respectful, the family functions better, can support each other better, and the world, especially our own place in it, is better. Respecting our elders brings us together and promotes harmony rather than driving us apart; and that is good. But just like all moral and religious teachings which contain general truths, there are exceptions. A parent who abuses his or her child does not earn nor deserve respect, and the moral principle does not apply. (Most people, of course, are not aware that these exceptions were in the really small print on the back of Moses' tablet.) To explain some traditional moral principles as an outgrowth of human beings having evolved as social and gregarious animals that cannot survive alone, can lead to just as much good behavior as religious guidelines embedded in theological commandments.

The best religious stories and myths easily connect to our current everyday experience but are also statements of timeless truths or eternal human struggles. Stories of a Great Flood are a good example. We have all seen floods, even if limited to television news reports. There are several different ancient recorded stories of a great flood emanating from different cultures and parts of the world, but the one that made it into the Judeo-Christian literature was the story of Noah and the ark. This story originated in the Mesopotamian River Valley between the two great rivers, the Tigris and the Euphrates, in what today is Iraq. If we are asked to believe as factual, Biblical stories like Noah rounding up two of every species of animal when the entire surface of the earth was about to be flooded, then part of the foundation for traditional Judeo-Christian beliefs has little to do with our current understanding of the world. In fact we can pretty confidently say, it probably didn't happen exactly the way the story is portrayed in the Bible.

Noah's isn't the only ancient story about great floods; but we can understand why this story would arise where it did in the Mesopotamian River Valley. If we lived in ancient times between huge rivers beyond which we had never traveled and they both flooded at once, it would seem that the whole world was flooded. It was a meaningful story for that time and that place with their limited understanding of their physical world. It is easy to see by looking at a map that heavy rains in this area could cause massive flooding between these two rivers. It would be easy for people who had never left this land to believe that their entire world was covered by water. After the fact, such a colossal event would naturally be assigned some theological or philosophical interpretation, just as we do today when we try to cope with natural disasters. Why did this happen? Which god was unhappy? If one God, why would "he" do this? Why did Noah and some animals survive, when everyone else perished? Over time the awe and fear of the massive forces of Nature's flood waters came to be interpreted as the wrath of God cleansing the Earth from its sins, or at least giving mankind a pretty thorough scrubbing. Not only the story but also the theological interpretation of why it happened should cause some serious questioning.

It does no harm to have small children in Sunday schools draw thousands of pictures of pairs of animals marching onto an ark—whatever that is. But for this and other ancient religious stories to apply to adult spirituality today, we must move beyond the most incredible, unbelievable, implausible parts of these religious teachings. After mankind evolved to inhabit the earth, it is unlikely it was all covered again in water. Nor did all species of animals live in one part of the world where they could have been gathered on a gigantic barge of some sort. We trivialize spirituality if we require believing the unbelievable or suggest that spiritual revelation is found primarily in outdated world-views.

The problem with many of these religious stories and myths is they make reference to symbolism and beliefs that we now know are impossible or for which we have totally lost the meaning or represent views we no longer embrace. Perhaps some biblical scholars can tell us what the meaning of salt was in the story of Lot's wife being turned into a pillar of salt when she disobeyed God (and her husband—which currently couldn't make it into any religious teachings because of political/gender incorrectness, Genesis 19:2). Did she get arthritis? Was there a pillar in the desert that tasted like salt? Religious teachings that require someone else interpreting for us are of limited value. How our ancestors experienced God is interesting, sometimes enriching, and ties us to a history of spiritual worshippers. Sometimes, however, the ancient stories are incomprehensible and simply get in the way of looking at our own spiritual experience and we need to replace them.

Modern Mythology

The beauty of modern scientific investigation and revelation is that everyone will get the same result with the same explanation. An experiment combining oxygen with iron taking place in China, produces the same results in India and the same explanation holds true whether it is done in Chinese or French, by an adult or child, by a Hindu or a Christian Scientist. It is a method of understanding that is only several hundred years old. It obviously was not necessary for the development of human societies nor the survival of the human race, but it also just as obviously and dramatically has affected the evolution and direction of human life on this planet. Scientific methods have brought about industrial and technological revolution, nuclear bombs, and genetic splicing. Scientific methodology and knowledge has and will continue to exert increasing force on the future of our planet. Fortunately the manifestations of God are revealed in the modern science lab just as much as through Moses, Mohammed, Buddha, and Confucius if we choose to see them. The explanations and stories that emerge from our scientific labs are also myths to some degree, limited by current knowledge and human intelligence itself, but they are more current stories of explanation and wonder and can make our current spiritual understanding more appropriate and more relevant for our time.

We can change the original meaning of the story of the Great Flood and reinterpret it with spiritual relevancy for today if we look at the story both concretely and symbolically at the same time. We have all felt utter despair, just drifting and enduring with no direction or solution, and then unexpectedly, wondrously there is hope. That is our human experience. The oral story-tellers shaped and perfected the story of Noah until it succinctly encapsulated inspiration and hope for both adults and children. For the most part today, we drop out the interpretation that this was God's punishment for the wickedness of humans. And no one includes in the story the difficulty of cleaning up the elephant dung or how the starving tigers had to eat some of the sheep to survive. We leave out some things and embellish other to create stories that speak to our core human feelings about safety, belonging, and significance. Each succeeding generation or culture needs and develops its own inspirational stories and sometime it is better to find new ones because they now are more powerful than reinterpreting the old ones. The humorous ones often seem to provide a special closeness to God. Did you hear the one about…

> There was this Iowa farmer who had done very well with his crops on the bottom-land next to the Mississippi River. You probably saw it on the nightly news. The rains came. The Mississippi started rising, and began to cover the road in front of his house. The local fire department came by in their truck with their big loudspeaker and called out:
>
> "You've got to get out now. The water is going to get even higher. We need to evacuate you."

The TV crew riding along, caught the farmer's reply on tape and replayed it on the evening news:
"No thanks. I've got faith. God will provide for me. I'm sticking it out!"

Well, the water did continue to rise, and on the news the next night the sheriff was now out in his boat, pulling up to the man's house with the water completely covering the first floor and the farmer hanging out his second story window. The sheriff calls out:
"You've got to get out now. The water is going to get even higher. We need to evacuate you, now!"

And the farmer calls back:
"I've got faith. God's going to provide for me. I'm staying here!"

Sure enough, the water got higher and higher and the next night the news camera showed the water lapping near the roof line and the farmer now sitting on top of his roof. The local Coast Guard helicopter from the Mississippi station hovers over the roof and lowers a basket. They call out over their loud speaker:
"You've got to get out now. The water is still coming up. You have to leave!"

> And you can read the farmers lips as he waves them off:
> "I've got faith. God will provide for me."
>
> For once the weather forecasters were right. The water did continue to rise and the farm house slowly rose off its foundation and tumbled over in the rushing water. The farmer was thrown into the water and disappeared beneath it.
>
> It turns out that the farmer was really a good old guy and he made it to Heaven. He hadn't been there but a few days when God came by with his orientation packet and asked if the farmer had any questions. The farmer said:
> "Well Sir, this is a really nice place you've got here. I like it a lot. Real nice! I did have just one little complaint I wanted to discuss with you, however. You know I always believed that if I had faith in you, you'd take care of me and protect me. Where were you?"
>
> God looked at him over the top of his bifocals (well, God was pretty old by now). And God said:
> "You've got a complaint? You think you have a complaint? I sent a truck, a boat, and a helicopter…!"

We can extrapolate various truths from this modern mythological Great Flood Story: God's presence is in the things around us. Don't ignore the possibilities life offers us. Take God's revelations as they present themselves. The love of God comes through our fellow human beings, etc. It's a cute story. It's contemporary. It's humorous. It has an underlying truth. It has lots of the things that make spiritual and religious metaphors enticing. It's as good or better than the Noah's Ark story. And yes, if God doesn't have a sense of humor, then She's really missing something and we'll be tempted to go back to the male myth.

Each succeeding generation understands more about the functioning of creation and reshapes their old knowledge to address the same continuing emotional and spiritual needs. We once believed Earth was the center of the universe, but we learned that Earth rotated around the sun. It didn't change our need to be loved and reassured. It caused a major reorganization of how we understand our place in creation, but not our desire and hope that we are special. We gave up, for the most part, explanations of events that were based primarily on supernatural concepts such as witches, angels, ghosts and gods because we could predict and explain most events through scientific understanding. There were just better explanations. We wouldn't be able to build cars and space ships if our explanation as to why things burn or combust was still confined to evil spells and spirits.

If someone told you they knew a guy down the street who claimed he could turn water into wine, like the story of Jesus in the Bible, would you believe it? Would you bet all the money you have that it is true or would you be better off buying a lottery ticket? Would you base a belief in a god on it? In fact not only would we not believe this story, but we would also tend to disbelieve anything else the guy had to say. We would be very skeptical of any other claims he made. It's obviously a hoax, a trick, or a lie. Based on our current understanding and experience of how the world works we wouldn't believe such a story unless he could demonstrate it many times under controlled scientific conditions. Our knowledge does not need to destroy our spiritual sensitivity. We just have to allow our knowledge to lead us to new spiritual and emotional understanding.

Seeking Truth With Human Consciousness

In the 17th century we did not understand how scientific knowledge could expand our understanding of our spiritual nature. So science was split off from emotional and spiritual studies. In fact scientific knowledge was seen as a threat to spirituality. It was this false but pragmatic agreement with the Catholic Church that kept Descartes and others from being excommunicated or arrested. He could study scientific knowledge because the spiritual and emotional dimension would remain the separate, unexamined domain of the Church. So the mold was cast for the two-dimensional mistake that assumed that science is unaffected by human consciousness and that spirituality and emotional issues are separate from physical matter and hard science. This false duality carries forward into current religions and churches. Highly trained people such as doctors, physicists, and chemists deal all week with highly predictable manipulation of scientific information, and for some reason worship on the weekends by talking about ancient mythological stories rather than the revelations of God they have seen in front of them the entire week.

It was the physicists who finally began to pull science, psychology, and metaphysics back together. They led the way for a new understanding of cosmology and hence provide a new platform for spiritual understanding. The quantum physicists came to understand that our scientific knowledge is shaped and limited by our consciousness and awareness. For instance, we cannot know both the position of an electron and its movement at the same time. We can only know one or the other at a time. In fact it is a potential whose properties are manifest to us only when we measure it. When we humans try to measure or observe things, other properties and potentials change. Our human conscious perception shapes the nature of what is and what can happen.

We have to relearn the inseparability of the knower from what is known, that energy and matter are different expressions of the same thing, that our minds and bodies are inseparable expressions of the same existence. These conundrums provide more than enough modern day mystery and knowledge to inspire spiritual reflection, moral debate, and current parables. We need not limit ourselves to those posed by our less knowledgeable ancestors. We really have a lot of catching up to do that will be addressed in later chapters. At the same time, however, we still have the useful ability to gain important understanding from our own mind.

Just as prophets of old had revelations when they sat under a fig tree or stared at a fire, we can do the same thing. The images, stories, and personal truths that emerge into our conscious mind from our unconscious mind and intuition can become part of our own personal spiritual library. We have all experienced altered states of consciousness that occasionally bring us insight or information. Think of the number of times when you have gone to bed with a dilemma or unsolved problem and the next morning you know the solution or have a new idea. Our conscious, intellectual, rational way of thinking is not the only way we can learn or get insight.

One of the techniques psychologists use to help people learn from their unconscious mind is to help them personify their unconscious knowledge and wisdom in visual imagery. For instance, we can imagine a loving, wise inner advisor who can talk with us, a modification of a memory of a real person who was especially kind, wise, and understanding or, unfortunately in my case, a smart-mouthed kid. "Mikey" is my somewhat flippant, arrogant, and playful inner self whom no one knows completely, including me; but he knows a lot of things I don't consciously know. He's both silly and wise because he never has to deal with the external world. Of course, Mikey, is also me; but in my fantasy and mental imagery, he seems separate. I was really serious about trying to get some insight about an important issue in my life when I attended a mental imagery workshop. I asked my "inner advisor" what I should do to manage my time and balance my life better. I was feeling somewhat torn between all the clinical and administrative duties I had and was feeling very unsettled.

As I settled into my fantasy, I found that Mikey wasn't taking this exercise nearly as seriously as I was. He was lounging around watching TV in his favorite overstuffed chair, just enjoying himself, as he seemed accustomed to doing, when I asked him for help with being too busy. Mikey got up from his chair and started walking toward the refrigerator to get a Coke. (The "real" me would deprive myself of my favorite drink in order to drink the cheaper generic stuff; but Noooo, not Mikey!) Over his shoulder he threw me a disdainful and dismissive reply:

"That's your problem. You go fix it. I've got better things to do."

I was offended and perplexed that my sensitive, caring, needing-to-be-loved-and-understood self had some blunt, smart-mouthed kid as my supposedly wise inner advisor. But upon reflection, I gained more from his advice. All the struggles about where I was going to put my time and energy were just choices. I could make them any time I wanted, any way I wanted. I just didn't want to give up anything. Further, it was clear that it was my responsibility as an adult to make these choices and quit complaining about how hard it was. And it wasn't really a big deal. Mikey wasn't about to feel unloved or stressed-out because I chose to get tired from working. Wouldn't even feel the least bit sorry for me!

This kind of personal, inner-active mental imagery that any of us can use, sounds very similar (with a little less dignity) to some of the revelations or conversations with God or spirit guides that in the past have sometimes been related as divine revelation. Whatever their source, all forms of mythological stories invite each of us to add our own interpretation and shape it to our own needs. This does not make myths untrue, but rather are stories that invite us to make them meaningful for ourselves.

The Nearly Famous Fable of the Fly and the Cow

Inspirational stories and meaning-inviting myths don't have to be sentimental, somber, hundreds of years old, or even serious. They aren't found only in designated religious texts, told by priests, or taught in religious schools. As an example, consider the nearly famous story of the fly and the cow:

> One time there was this fly just looking for his next meal. As he was buzzing through a pasture, he landed on the backside of a cow. He wasn't sure whether this particular rest stop had good food, so he taste-tested it by chomp'n down real hard on that cow's behind. Now the cow, she was half dozing after munching down on a truly outstanding patch of grass, just pasteurizing away in the shade of a lone acorn tree on a hot afternoon. But when that fly bit her, she jumped clean off the ground. She whipped her tail around intending to jump-start that fly on the way to Eternity. Unfortunately, her tail whacked her sister right in the eye. Some say this was the beginning of the whole Mad Cow Disease thing. You see, her sister had been carrying on a right good snooze, dreaming about the bull on the other side of the barn. So she jumped up, and

she snorted, and she bellowed, and fell into her cousin who was startled right out of her afternoon prayers. Well, this started a chain reaction of jumping and snorting and carrying on from one cow to the next, so loud that they all thought something terrible was happening. So they all started running, and snorting, and carrying on; except, of course, for the first cow who just wanted to go back to sleep now that the fly was gone.

But the rest of them took off runn'n scared. A whole stampede, each cow running because the cow beside her was. And they were breathing pretty heavy by now, and sweating, and getting tired. But the fear kept driving them on. Right toward the electric fence over by the highway! You know the kind, where you touch it and get about a gizillion volts clear through you and it will even keep elephants corralled. But this time those cows hit that fence straight on, doing well, probably over maybe 10 mile an hour; but with a lot of beef behind it! They went clean through that fence like it wasn't there. So intent were they on escaping danger that they didn't feel the barbed wire tear through their skin and the gizillion volts only charged their fear up even more. All they felt was the roar of their terror in their ears and the fear in their bellies.

That is, until they reached the highway. Now, it was election season and all the politicians were out hunting votes. And wouldn't you know, the fellar with the nice hair, who everyone just knew was going to be the next president, just happened to be politicking down that road at about 70 miles an hour. Some of those cows gallumped on across the road just fine. Some of them saw that caravan barreling down on them with the CIA, the FBI, and the bugs on the windshield and they were so scared that they forgot what they were runn'n from and turned back. All except one. So there she was, the cow in the headlights. Could not move! No, sir. And bang! That crash was so loud that even that first sleepy cow over under the tree turned to look. Knocked that undecided, non-voting cow clear over into the ditch, dead. And they discovered the fellar with the nice hair over in the other ditch dead; but the cows didn't really spend too much time thinking about that, especially that first cow who now had gone completely back to sleep.

Verily I say unto you, my brothers and sisters: don't stampede, when life has only bitten you on the behind!

Spirits, Angels, and Other Supernatural Experiences

> Body and soul are not two different things,
> but only two ways of perceiving the same thing.
> Similarly, physics and psychology are only
> different attempts to link our experiences together
> by way of systematic thoughts.
> (Albert Einstein, the Human Side.
> H. Dukas and B. Hoffmann, eds.)

Most people have never seen an angel, nor have most of us met space aliens, dead ancestors, gods, or spirits that don't have material bodies. Except for the occasional story or testimonial of an encounter with beings without bodies, there is no scientific evidence for such existence and no impact on our everyday life. If something like non-material beings exist, they are essentially irrelevant to our daily existence. Our interest in non-material beings is ultimately a question about ourselves: Are we humans essentially a non-material spirit that wanted to find a body in order to have a human experience? Or, are we humans essentially a material body that can consciously detect and formulate a spiritual connection between us and the rest of creation?

The problem with Western theological concepts is the same as with science. Intellectually we separated feeling and consciousness from fact and matter. Theology relies heavily on personal emotional needs and science relies heavily on reason. Western religious teachings often lean toward the concept of a god actively intervening to change the course of human events. But most Americans no longer believe that an angry force somewhere is after us when lightening strikes during a thunderstorm or that evil spirits are lurking about to intervene in the events of our day. Today, if we could even hear a potential predator walking around our air-conditioned homes, we'd call Critter Control or simply take a gun and kill the beast who dared wander onto our turf. The idea of non-material beings, spirits, and gods are not a part of our life experience or belief system. Yet much religious thought, upon which our very reason for being is explained, rests on the core concept of a central non-material being.

Quite in contrast to the rest of their beliefs, many people in American culture currently choose to attribute good and joyful occurrences to guardian angels or God's will and bad occurrences to unexplained luck or natural forces. We praise God for the birth of a child, surviving an accident, or even a sports victory. Few people blame God for the child with birth defects, the loss of a friend in an accident, or failure to be victorious on our job or other playing field. The emergence of monotheism, the idea of their being only one god, created a major theological and intellectual dilemma. Before monotheism the multitude of competing gods could be used to explain both good events and bad: victories and losses in battle, fertility, weather changes, and so on, depending on the mood of the gods and the appeasing or offending actions of human subjects. Except for a few people who still explain things as "the work of the Devil", we have given up explaining bad events as the action of unseen beings or gods. Supernatural explanations today seem to flow more often when we receive something positive that we didn't work for, deserve, expect, or control. When we experience an uplifting moment, when we can't believe we can be so lucky or feel so good by anything we did, we are more likely to attribute it to a supernatural cause though there is no more evidence for kind, protective spiritual beings than there is for mean, dangerous non-material beings.

A Personal Experience With an Angel?

I've always liked wilderness camping—in the Everglades, in the Minnesota and Canadian North Woods, the Appalachian Trail, the Rocky Mountains, any place where you're completely on your own. Life is very simple then. With only what you can take with you on foot, horseback, or canoe, can you stay warm and dry for a week or two? Can you eat? Can you sleep comfortably? Can you keep from getting eaten—by bugs or something larger? Can you take care of yourself, where there is no shelter, no technology and no help? Can you keep from getting lost? Can you get back? It sometimes takes much of the day just to accomplish these basics of moving from one place to another and surviving. The day's tasks are immediately rewarded and meaningful—or not. In the wilderness life's meaning is very pure and clear: If you stay alive, there is no unfinished business. Everything else you do, is just optional—very useful training for living in the "real" world back home. With children and increasing complexity to plan these trips, wilderness experiences have become fewer and farther apart in our family; but we will never forget The Bear.

We found a wrangler in the appropriately named Bear Tooth Mountains who was willing to take us over a couple of mountain passes by horseback, drop us off, and come back in a week with the horses to pick us up. Planning food and gear in the Midwest, transporting it by plane to Denver, and hauling it over winding hill hugging dirt roads to the ranch while meeting everyone's "must take" list and keeping under the weight limit for the pack horses was the usual major challenge. But having done this kind of thing several times, we felt we could easily manage this. That's probably why we left one bag of our gear on the curb at the Denver airport as we excitedly threw almost everything into the rental van. An unplanned stop at WalMart replenished our losses and our spirits.

After snaking our way up into the mountains through an Indian reservation, we found the ranch and camped for a night nearby under stars that canopied forever. "Have you ever ridden before?" We quickly calculated that the zoo pony rides and a pack trip 15 years previously probably weren't what they meant. The tip off was that they all wore sweaty cowboy hats, and the boot cut jeans, and walked not only with bowed legs but with limps in both legs, and their cowboys boots were really scuffed up and dirty. And the horses were not your pony ride, sweaty one ton weaklings. These horses were jumping and dancing and wouldn't behave even for this 270 pound massive wrangler who could lift a bale of hay in one hand and throw a horse sideways with the other. Fear quickly overcame pride, and we admitted that our experience with horses was somewhat, shall we say, "limited".

After the usual tears and family conference over who got to ride Baldy or Smoky Joe or Bear Bait, we set off with great anticipation. It was a long climb, with many switch-backs, over two mountain passes, seeing not another living soul, until we found our lake destination late in the afternoon. We said good-bye to the wrangler and the horses and set up camp. Hiking, fishing, exploring. Each day improving the campsite and venturing off in new directions. Tying things down for storms that never come when you're ready, but for which being unprepared always brings misery. The children created elaborate games in the flowering meadows. I strung the ropes ever higher between two trees in order to hang the food out of the reach of any wandering bears or mountain lions. A life filled with easy purpose and peace.

Then one night after the two younger ones were just asleep, we heard the thumping and snorting of The Bear. We were initially almost calm. (OK, OK, so I was just pretending.) Not only was the food fifty yards away, ten feet off the ground, but it was suspended in mid-air, hanging from a rope hanging from another rope strung between two trees. He'll <u>never</u> get it! And, we even had a back up plan; but it's amazing how good your hearing and imagination becomes when it's pitch black, there's a gigantic bear outside, and the only thing between you and The Bear are a few threads of nylon tent! We heard him snorting and pawing the ground. Some walking around. A <u>lot</u> of huffing. Clawing up a tree. Thumping back to the ground with a plop. We're feeling pretty clever—he can't get the food! Wait a minute! If he can't get the food…will he come over HERE?

Plan B rested on the waterproof tin of firecrackers we always carry just for an emergency such as this. So we lit off a string. The only good part of that was, somehow it didn't wake up the younger ones and didn't set the tent on fire. It must have been Bear Independence Day or something, because he seemed to enjoy the show. It probably gave him more light to see the food bag because The Bear, now having worked on this project for at least half an hour, also developed a back up plan. We heard him working his way up the other tree from which the rope was strung. Then we heard a giant THUD! He's got the food!

Now this finally gave me something reassuring I could say to my wife and son…and myself: "Well, he won't be coming over here. He's got what he wants!" (I hope, I hope, I hope). Much to our relief, not only did that turn out to be true, but we also learned that one seemingly pathetically small canister of propane will keep your camp light burning the entire night—at least if you stay awake to watch it. You know how they say there's hardly anything more spectacular than the sun when it pops up over the mountains in the morning? We are a family who can personally vouch for that!

So here we are safe and sound. We are, aren't we? Miles from nowhere. Over two mountain passes. With no food. And The Bear, who has just located a new supermarket with give-away prices right in our back yard. I convince my 10 year old son that it will be <u>fun</u> to go look at what The Bear did to our food. (Well, you didn't expect me to go up there alone, did you?) With nonchalant boisterousness we strolled the fifty yards up the mountain. There is not a trace of anything! No food bag. No garbage. No scraps. Only a broken rope hanging like a gallows between the two trees. The Bear obviously did a nearly perfect swan dive (deduction for the landing) from the tree onto our food bag, broke the rope, and then took it somewhere. We edge our way up, unable to see what is lurking behind the next boulder—making lots of noise. We find some things! A bag ripped to shreds. Tin cans crushed with giant teeth marks ripping them open. Carefully opened candy wrappers everywhere. Drink mixes licked clean. But a jelly jar that somehow was only wounded by bear slobber...and some crackers in a tin box...and there's an apple! We pack up our gear for the wrangler to pick up later, improvise a carrying sling from a jacket for the four year old, and start down the trail with a lot of loud talking and backward glances. We know we're going to be O.K. now. It will just be a long challenging day's hike out.

Very surprisingly we encounter three travelers that day. The first couple is camped a mile or so away and we warn them about The Bear. We later step to the side as a string of lamas unexpectedly pick their way up the trail, loaded down with the gear of their campers. Late in the day we again step to the side and wave to a lone rider on a beautiful black horse coming up the trail. No one passes us coming out of the mountains on the single narrow trail. When we finally reach the trail head, we are surprised to meet the ranch owner with a string of horses—our horses. Where was she going?

A lone rider on a beautiful black horse whom she didn't know and had never seen before came by the ranch (in an area where neighbors are a whole lot more scarce then bald eagles and everyone knows your horse by its first name). The rider didn't dismount, but simply told her that the family she had up in the mountains had some trouble and needed help; and then he rode off. So she set off to find us. The next morning after she had rescued our gear (in the dark), we sat on the porch and talked some more.

Yes, there is only one way to get in or out of the mountains, on this single trail. No, no one passed us coming out—certainly not the rider on horseback we encountered. We never told anyone we needed help. We never even talked to the rider who passed us coming up the trail on the black horse. Even if he had talked to the camped couple many miles back in the mountains we had seen in the morning, how could he get all the way in to find them and back out of the mountains without passing us—and with so much time that she had saddled 8 horses and trucked them to the trail head before we got there? The rider would have had to be miles away at the ranch even before we met him on the trail.

I don't believe in guardian angels. I don't believe in guardian angels. I don't believe in guardian angels! Well, maybe we'll have ponder this mystery a bit longer…

For some this would be enough evidence. In a highly emotional state, experiencing relief, grateful for unexpected help, lacking clear explanation, it is enticing to jump the gap of concrete evidence and say this was a divine, other-worldly, intervention. Maybe it was.

We'd all feel better if we had a guardian angel, or even if we could just interpret events as though we did. But for some of us, the gift and burden of intellectual thought and examination does not allow this as sufficient evidence of other worldly beings. For some who believe more strongly in spirit beings, this might be totally convincing. Certainly during that 24 hour period we experienced something very much out of the ordinary. The lone rider adds even more mystery in the midst of an unforgettable experience. I am grateful both for the safety of my family and the experience of curious wonderment. If this was the appearance of a spirit, or a projection of our own emotional needs shaping reality, I am equally appreciative of it, and still am in wonder. And you know what else? We never actually saw The Bear in the blackness. Was it a spirit also?

Experiences That Lead to Supernatural Interpretation

Larry LeShan, who has written creatively and dynamically on human consciousness cites research and his own experience that some humans, at least occasionally, obtain knowledge and have experiences that go beyond our everyday experience, including mental telepathy and psychokinesis. Even in these situations, however, the role of human consciousness controls the experience. LeShan and others spent many hours working with a psychic, Eileen Garrett, under research conditions. She would go into a trance, contact a spirit personality, speak in a voice and speech pattern identified as that of a deceased person about whom someone was asking questions, and reveal personal information that only the questioning person should have known.

> ...Rosalind Heywood told me of the time when she was interviewing Mrs. Garrett who was in trance and speaking as if she were "Abdul Latif," her second major spirit control.
> Mrs. Heywood is a very gifted psychic herself as well as one of the wisest and most widely learned people in psychical research. She decided to use her own, highly developed paranormal abilities to perceive "Abdul Latif." She said, "I put out antennae and it seemed to me that he only existed for the subject under discussion."
> ...The spirit control enables us to externalize and use paranormal information and abilities. It solves the problem of living with the idea that I have information whose source I do not know, and that I could not possibly have since I believe that the only valid reality is the sensory reality. It also enables me to use psychokinetic abilities in a way that does not cause my anxiety and unbelief to immediately block them. (Lawrence LeShan, Alternate Realities.)

Some people, due to their personal sensitivities or what they were raised to expect, encounter or interpret experiences of intuitive knowledge as communication with non-material personalities. This was illustrated by a young woman who told me her experience. Over the years, she had a somewhat vague series of physical symptoms. Her medical tests were suggesting something wrong, but very difficult to diagnose, perhaps some form of autoimmune disease. But her goal was to have children. Her doctors strongly recommended that she not get pregnant since they were fearful that it would harm her own health. Over time she had become gradually aware of her ability occasionally to see auras around people and have strong intuitive knowledge of the unconscious emotional energy of other people. In her explorations of these experiences, she visited a spiritual healer who felt there was an energy blockage around her ovaries which was related to her inability to get pregnant. With or without the help of the medical professionals and this spiritual healer she eventually not only delivered one child but became pregnant a second time.

By this time she had met a priest who also experienced some of these intuitive impressions. Together they shared an awareness over an hour period of the presence of a being who was extremely sad, who felt unable to be born. They both interpreted this to be related to her pregnancy. She shared her love and her grief with this presence. The next morning she miscarried. While she felt immense sadness, she also felt grateful for the opportunity to have communicated her acceptance and love to this soul, whether or not it could be born.

These kinds of experiences are not, for many, hard evidence of non-material beings nor spiritual entities, but enough people report these sorts of experiences that we must accept that some or all of us have the ability to intuit knowledge and to experience things outside our normal thinking and sensory processes. We may shape our intuitive knowledge into the form of other worldly personalities in order to help us understand or clarify the experience, or mentally project ourselves outside our body to help formulate unconscious knowledge. For this mother, the encounter with an unborn being may have been a projection of her own feelings when her unconscious mind realized she was miscarrying. It may be that this priest has a very finely tuned awareness of the feelings and unconscious physical working of other people. It was a deeply moving experience and was appreciated as a spiritual experience and emotional resolution to the loss of her unborn child.

Another kind of very personal and powerful experience with non-material beings is reported in “near death experiences” (NDE). There is a certain commonality among some of these experiences. When the human body is unconscious and dying, some common thought patterns and interpretations of the experience are apparently sometimes remembered—if the people are successfully resuscitated or recover. These people often report a sense of being dead, of being outside their body and a reluctance to return, often accompanied by a life review, and a wonderful assurance of peace and calmness often conveyed in the form of a white light or other spiritual presence that removes any concerns about their mortal existence. They sometimes have the experience of choosing to move on toward that loving presence or returning to their former existence. These experiences are often accompanied by a sense of peace, an out of body experience that allows them to see not only their own dead body and people trying to resuscitate them, but sometimes seeing events in other places, other people, religious figures or God. It sounds like a pretty wonderful and exciting experience that all of us might enjoy except that it is a very high risk activity: we have to die to have the experience.

But not everyone who is resuscitated reports a wondrous near-death experience. Some remember nothing. In fact some have lost significant portions of their memory. Melvin Morse, who reports hundreds of these experiences in Children of the Light and Transformed by the Light, cites research that suggests these experiences are linked to a lack of oxygen to the right temporal lobe of the brain. The interpretation of this experience of dying is created through both our unconscious and conscious mind. It becomes an experience we shape to fit our thought patterns in order to understand it. Morse points out how cultural influences shape the event:

> In Japan, a study of four hundred near-death experiences reveals that many of them see long dark rivers and beautiful flowers. Indians sometimes see heaven as a giant bureaucracy and are frequently sent back because of clerical errors. Americans and the English are usually sent back for love or to do a job while the natives of Micronesia say that the heaven they see is similar to a large, brightly lit American city with loud noisy cars and tall buildings...Many...African people interpreted the event as somewhat evil. Half of the participants in this simple study thought NDE signified that they were "bewitched" or about to be. Another called it a "bad omen".

(Melvin Morse: Transformed by the Light.)

We are drawn to these NDE stories because of the dramatic miraculous recoveries and the curiosity we have about what happens when we die. We apparently can't ever know whether these stories contain any information about what really happens after we are dead, since we can't get any reports from people who stayed dead and did not recover. It is logical that even at the unconscious level our interpretation of what happens is shaped by the limitations of our brain anatomy as well as by our cultural learning and do not represent what happens when our bodies are completely dead and we have no more basis for conscious thought or interpretation.

"Medical intuitives" such as Edgar Caycee or more currently such as Caroline Myss and others seemingly sometimes tap information channels that seem to sometimes allow them some knowledge of the health of another person's body even if they are hundreds of miles away. Some of these healers or receivers of knowledge imagine they are going through a third party, sometimes thought of as God, angels, or other mediums. Some directly access some source of knowledge, but they all tend to claim this and any healing that may then occur comes from something beyond their everyday sense of themselves. Most of us have little experience like this in our lifetime and people with these psychic abilities are very few in number and not always accurate in their perceptions. There is, however, some more scientific evidence that human consciousness can affect non-conscious material objects. Studies at the Princeton University Engineering Anomalies Research Laboratory showed that we humans, through mental concentration, can deliberately affect the random generation of impulses by a micro-electronic generator. (Robert Jahn and Brenda Dunne. Margins of Reality.) Perhaps all of us have some small ability in this area.

It may be that some individuals experience things or communicate with energy and forces in the universe the rest of us aren't aware of. In that case, the rest of us have to be curious, open to the possibility of our own enlightenment, but proceed with our lives as though there were no outside beings or forces affecting us because we simply don't experience it. It doesn't make those of us without supernatural experiences less reverent or spiritual, perhaps just less interesting. Some day the Universe might also entertain us with a glimpse of some other dimension of reality. In the meantime our spirituality cannot rest on the experiences of others or what we haven't seen and don't know. What each of us does experience, however, is hopefully more than enough to maintain appreciation, wonder, and reverence.

Our Physiology Determines Our Reality

Human beings tend to personalize and personify our experiences of the Infinite in human form because there really is no other choice. If we sense something, we're not going to interpret it like a bumble bee, a fish, or an earth worm would. If we experience thirst we seek a stream, well, faucet, or bottle from which to drink. We don't eat our way deeper into the soil in search of more moisture. When we want to have babies, we think it's logical to go to visit the doctor and the baby store instead of jumping in the ocean and swimming several thousand miles to find our birthplace, or navigate by memories of magnetic fields and sights and smells to nest in far away places. Each species and each individual experiences and perceives the wonders of the of the Universe and connects to the Infinite in its own special ways.

We have a built in bias to assume that the source of creation has human characteristics and a personality just like us. Because we have to trust our own senses, some of our strongest experiences and perceptions lead us to inaccurate beliefs. Although sight and personal experience would clearly lead us to the conclusion that the world is flat, we finally proved to ourselves otherwise. We're currently getting more serious about trying to discover life forms elsewhere in the universe after ignoring or not wanting to believe that possibility. This will further force us to look at the nature of what we think is real and possible. Our views change as we learn that what we thought was true is altered by new knowledge. Those changes sometimes run counter to our experience and mostly deeply held beliefs.

Every year a multitude of birds enjoys the woods surrounding our home. Each summer a few of them die or get serious headaches and lie dazed on the ground for awhile when they fly full speed into the reflection of the woods in our windows. Like the birds our understanding of reality is always limited by our current knowledge, experience, perception, and understanding. It's almost as hard to convince a human being that God doesn't have human qualities as it would be to convince a bird it had crashed into a woods that wasn't there. All humans, just as all other species, inherit ways of perceiving and knowing our surroundings that influence what we think reality can be.

Presumably worms perceive the world and the meaning of life differently from human beings—or don't have the capacity to do either. When I was in graduate school, one of the very few studies that stuck in my mind from experimental psychology was one with worms. Don't ask why (maybe their budget for hiring rats and college sophomores was cut), but someone decided to train worms to "run" a maze. There were many interesting experiments around this time which helped demonstrate behavioral and personality development. Researchers showed that humans and other animals learn to do and act according to what behavior is rewarded or punished. They discovered that if you put a reward at the end of a maze, rats, chickens and all the rest of us animals quickly learn the way to the prize and will keep going that direction time after time. Similarly, if we electrify the floor and give the animals a mild shock when they go the wrong direction, they learn and remember not to go that way—just like we now train dogs to stay in an enclosed area with an invisible electric fence. This behavioral learning theory was applied to explain why people go to their jobs and how they might become great authors, presidents, or criminals—through a series of rewards and punishments.

In an experimental group, the worms were successfully taught to turn one direction or another in a maze. These results were compared to a group of underprivileged, uneducated worms who apparently wandered aimlessly through life. Through statistical comparison, the researchers demonstrated that the educated group had learned to turn the chosen direction, and it wasn't just chance or luck. As it turned out, however, good luck was not the fortune at the end of the maze for some of these college-educated worms. The experimenters took some of their most accomplished and educated worms, put them through a grinder and fed them to another generation of worms. (How's school going, son? Great, dad! I'm timing the worms. Next semester, I think I'll get to move up to Blender!)

But wait! Before we get too preoccupied with the wisdom of spending our money on sending our children to ivory towers with professors whose heads may be focused well below ground, or the ethics of grinding up worms, watch that new generation of worms run the maze. They weren't taught anything about it, but they tend to turn the specified direction just like their dead ancestors. They have some knowledge they didn't learn! (R.A. Wilson and G.D. Collins. "Establishment of a Classically Conditioned Response and Transfer of Training via Cannibalism in Planaria". Perceptual Motor Skills, 1967, 24, 727-30). While the validity of this experiment has been challenged, like almost all others that produce unexpected results, hopefully no one will try to replicate it with human beings. We must entertain the possibility, however, that humans also can store and transfer information at an unconscious genetic level and that the learning from one generation can partially pass on to the next. Unconscious knowledge is clearly transferred from one generation to the next such as genetic susceptibility to certain diseases or inherited abilities in art or music. We need to consider that the level of our spiritual interest and sensitivity may also ultimately be a DNA or cellular based trait as well.

Ernest Rossi and others have helped conceptualize how information that is learned at a conscious level in human beings is transmitted, not only to brain cells that allow conscious knowledge, memory and awareness, but also transmitted unconsciously to every other cell in the body, even altering DNA information. (Ernest Rossi and David Cheek. Mind -Body Therapy.) We can now understand the neurochemistry of how the mind and body communicate with each other. In so doing we also come to understand again that the mind and body are just different manifestations of the same thing and that the artificial division we chose to make between the two needs to be discarded. More importantly, however, is to recognize that our knowledge, our mind, far exceeds the information available in our brains and our consciousness.

We can now see through our microscopes, the same receptor sites in our immune system for the neurochemicals that in the brain allow us to have conscious thought. In other words, the same chemical messengers that allow conscious thought communicate with the unconscious parts of our physiology—our unconscious mind. Not only is every piece of information to make another you, exactly like you, stored in the DNA of a single cell of your body, but also the unconscious information stored in your cells can be modified by new experiences, both conscious and unconscious. We count on this, for instance, when we give immunizations to prevent small pox or measles. We know our unconscious cellular memory will remember this new information about a foreign invader, create a solution for it, store that information, and kill that germ when it tries to invade our body. We are now also able to show that permanent changes in our physical body such as plaque build up on artery walls is affected by conscious mental factors such as anger and stress.

It takes a moment or two to adjust our thinking to the fact that our mind is not confined to the brain, and that the larger part of our knowledge and mind is not in our consciousness at all. We have oversimplified to divide the human being into mind and body and relegate the mind to being primarily a derivative function of the brain. We have oversimplified when we think our consciousness is our connection to God and that God is limited to a non-material human like consciousness. Our ability to think and then believe that we are separate from the "outside world" is a function of our particular brain anatomy, but it may or may not help us understand "reality".

Human Perception of the Infinite

It seems appropriate to try to integrate our understanding of the human conscious and unconscious mind with our understanding of spirituality. Unconscious information transfer helps explain how humans interact with the knowledge pool of the Universe. If Spirit is what we call the collective energizing, creating, and knowledge base of the universe, as well as our individual manifestation of it, then spirituality is simply being aware of our participation in and connection to this unifying entity of the universe. Spirituality does not rest on whether there are non-material personalities such as angels, god(s), or devil(s). It rests on whether there is a basic unity which connects and infuses all being. Before creation there was nothing and, at the same time, all possibility. After creation there is both created material substance and the diffusion of the Unity. In the part of existence we can know, human beings apparently are capable of a physical as well as a conscious awareness of our connection to the Common Existence Giving Source.

An encounter with spirits, angels and other non-material beings is probably a manifestation and projection of our own consciousness and emotions, incorporating our sense of things beyond ourselves and shaped by our human personality and ways of comprehending. Just because the abilities and limitations of our minds shape reality so we can understand it does not make it any less meaningful or real to the individual who experiences a connection to the All. Whether a person is color-blind or has an artist's gift for seeing and appreciating details of form and nuances of color, both people see something. We can only perceive with what we've got. We encounter the Unifying Spirit in our own personal, human way. It can be rational and logical. It can be physical calmness. It can be a simple sense of peace or an intense emotional feeling of being loved that brings tears to our eyes, joy to our hearts, and transformation to our lives. How we apprehend our spiritual connection or whether we explain it with other-worldly or secular language is not important. We all do the best we can to understand and describe our limited perception and understanding of the Infinite. What is important is whether our understanding and experience of spirituality helps give meaning and direction to our living. Does it touch our emotion, express a reassurance of our belonging here, does it shape what we do today and tomorrow?

As part of my introduction to adolescence, I went to church camp for several years. Besides learning things about sexuality I never would have learned at home, my favorite time was the Friday night campfires. These were out in the wooded grounds, with twinkling stars reminding us of the incomprehensible vastness of the universe coupled with the trance inducing flickers of campfire flames. There were quiet songs of Kum-by-ya. Some words of Jesus and God's love. And every time, an intense fullness in my mind, my heart, my throat and my eyes. I knew God's presence. He was there. I felt God. I talked to God.

God was a very personal being for me then in a way that probably can never be again. My mind began to learn too much, think too much, know too much, and question too much for these religious experiences to remain the same. It is no longer possible for me to think of God as limited to such a simple entity as a human consciousness. The intense feelings of needing to belong and be loved remain the same, however. I still have a sense of the Transcendent under a canopy of stars, so much so that my children tire of hearing my same inexplicable exclamations of joy and wonder that some of those stars we're seeing are so far away in time and space that they don't even exist any more. It is sad in some ways, but I can no longer think of this emotional experience as really communicating with a human like, non-material person, maybe even with a beard, rocking quietly in a heavenly place. I still experience and appreciate this awareness of connection and can feel my belonging, and the feeling of peace and joy that goes with that belonging and acceptance. The difference is that I now believe that my own consciousness and physiology are the key ingredient of both the need for and the experience of God as a personality. Letting spiritual concepts evolve and change is very hard sometimes, especially when our childlike needs of wanting to be accepted and appreciated by a loving parent figure are never outgrown. We can retain a sense of personal and spiritual attachment to the Infinite, however, without having to divorce the experience from scientific knowledge and the analytical portions of our mind.

If we envision or encounter non-material beings only because our own human personality is projected onto our vague experience of the Infinite, there is still a core of information and matter independent of our perception. It is our consciousness that gives it shape and meaning. The idea that not only our perception of reality but even the existence of reality is always shaped and determined by our own consciousness and perceptions is disconcerting to some because it always leaves the true nature of reality uncertain. For some it seems irreverent to say God has no understandable form until we humans envision it. It may be somewhat frightening or arrogant to conclude that life has no meaning until we envision what it is. Without human consciousness, however, we have no evidence that there is any consciousness at all, nor anyone to direct or care why we are here.

It probably doesn't matter how we experience or express our connection to the Collective Infinite. If we have any sense that we are connected, we find an intellectual and emotional way to satisfy our essential spiritual itch. It is not as personally comforting or reassuring to think that there is a Universal Existence of which we are a manifestation, as it is to think that a kindly grand-fatherly/motherly like god, out beyond the clouds a bit, personally thought us up and decided to give us birth. If our spiritual formulations are to be intellectually honest, however, we have to be able to integrate what we know scientifically about how the universe functions with our philosophical and religious explanations.

Human consciousness and emotional needs have a tendency to shape our God into the ultimate teddy bear, loving mother, or an eternal holy presence which personally embraces us. We long to directly experience our connection. We don't want to feel alone, without purpose or direction, without help! We want to feel that the universe would not be the same without us, that we are special, that in the billions of years of history of space and time, and even before that, it matters that we exist, that our individuality is recognized, that the "very hairs of our head our numbered". When we become aware of our individual connection to the All, we not only feel a part of it, we create a new dimension of God. So if we have to give up our concept of a personal God as our deliberate creator, we can replace it with the realization that <u>we human beings are the conscious mind of God on Earth</u>. Humans are created from God's image, and God is created in our image, each inseparable from the other.

We did not lose our spiritual faith when we found out that Earth wasn't the center of universe but is in fact only a rather small, obscure planet that goes around one of millions of suns. We can also adjust to the probability that a single or many non-material, super-human-like beings didn't create and aren't directing the on-going affairs and evolution of life on Earth. We humans may be here only by chance but also as a remarkable special conscious manifestation of All of Creation. In that brief time we call our lives, we are an expression of the physical presence and of the conscious mind of God on this planet. Let us live to honor and make the most of this precious, sacred, awe-inspiring moment.

Creation and Other Questions of Where Babies Come From

The smallest object that we can see, even under a microscope, contains millions of atoms. To see the atoms in a baseball, we would have to make the baseball the size of the earth. If a baseball were the size of the earth, its atoms would be about the size of grapes. If you can picture the earth as a huge glass filled with grapes, that is approximately how a baseball full of atoms would look…It would be impossible to see the nucleus of an atom the size of a grape. In fact, it would be impossible to see the nucleus of an atom the size of a room. To see the nucleus of an atom, the atom would have to be as high as fourteen-story building! The nucleus of an atom as high as a fourteen-story building would be about the size of a grain of salt. Since a nuclear particle has about 2,000 times more mass than an electron, the electrons revolving around this nucleus would be about as massive as dust particles!
(Gary Zukav: The Dancing Wu Li Masters.)

Beyond the Old Beginning

In the beginning Everything was One. No differentiation. No matter, no energy, no space, no time, no life, no being, no consciousness. Only potential and the possibility of everything. Various people have named it. God seems like a good name.

And then it flew apart and that which was a perfect unity of all that there is, was never whole again. Eventually, after several billion years, on this one undistinguished, rather small planet, in a small galaxy somewhere in space, several million light years from its nearest cousin galaxy which might sustain similar life—oceans and trees and salamanders grew and—of all things, can you believe it—furless creatures that walk on only two legs!

What was the purpose of this creation? God had an itch? God was bored? Being the All, having the All isn't enough? To think that the All had a reason to create something when God already had and was everything goes beyond human comprehension. Perhaps something went wrong, or was lacking, or was imperfect in the All, or there was an accident. To think that God consciously created the universe just so we humans could have our own little planet to exist on is pretty egotistical, but endearingly, that is our human nature. We also tend to think that human beings are somehow closer to and more like God than are rocks or snakes and other earthly creations. We even tend to think that we are the most important things in the universe. This focus on their own self importance could only develop in creatures that developed more brain cells than they really need just to survive, so they have a few million left over to ponder the philosophical importance and purpose of their own existence. Just because we have the ability and time to ponder why creation happened, doesn't necessarily justify concluding that all of creation was designed to be a special playground just for humans.

To say that a god with a human-like personality created everything seems too limiting. Not even humans, who admittedly do some pretty weird things, would try to create a Universe by first blowing themselves up. We certainly wouldn't sit around for several billion years waiting for something to grow. So either God is not like us, because he/she/it is much more patient and plans a lot longer into the future than we do (by several billion years), or God only takes on human characteristics when we human observers become aware of our place in and connection to the vastness of creation. It's pretty exciting that each of us came into being, but it hardly seems important to the survival and evolution of God and creation that any particular individual, including you and me, came into existence. Hard as it is to admit, the universe could probably have limped along somehow without me, and probably without you too, although the latter is a little less certain, of course. But the universe could also have survived without human beings at all—and did for billions of years. Something else would have evolved if humans hadn't, and something else probably has evolved elsewhere in the universe. The ability of the Collective Expansion to organize itself, reorganize itself, and eventually develop awareness of knowledge, planning, reflection, and contemplation of itself may have developed in many different non-human forms elsewhere in the universe.

But we humans cherish personal expressions and experience of our connection to the All. We want to be the "clay molded by His

Hands". Not since early Babylonian days have many people really believed we're actually made from clay. But to make this declaration about the nature of humans does not feel inaccurate when we recognize it as a metaphorical expression of our intuitive sense that we came from All Creation. To recognize that Biblical creation stories are myths or metaphorical expressions causes some people to feel that the whole foundation of their spiritual faith has been attacked. Scientific knowledge didn't exist for several thousand more years when our ancestors thought up these explanations, so they reflected the knowledge level and symbols of that time and culture. Biblical, pre-Biblical, and non-Biblical creation stories are plentiful. They include explanations that humans are descendants of an ash tree (Scandinavian) and that we are transformed from insects which stuck to the decaying giant body of P'an Ku who separated heaven and earth (Chinese). When we hear some of these unfamiliar accounts, it is easier to recognize them as ancient metaphors than it is to recognize the limitations of our own cultural and historical metaphors.

Many current religions do not recognize that their creation stories were mythological and metaphorical even when they were first thought up around campfires centuries before there was even written language. Eventually some of them got written down, such as the creation stories in the biblical book of Genesis. Many Christian churches still repeat the Biblical creation story as though it were an explanation of scientific fact rather than an expression of the heart and wonderment of the mind—or they just uncomfortably increasingly ignore it. Using pre-scientific mythology to explain that the world was created in seven days is like someone claiming my daughter wears plates on her face when I was trying to say that her eyes got as big as saucers. We confuse ourselves and weaken spiritual appreciation when we try to use poetic and metaphorical language to describe things better explained by scientific processes. The language of wonderment and poetry is beautiful, but it is not the language to try scientifically to explain how things happen or the natural order of the universe. Metaphorical and poetic language does not explain well why an airplane falls out of the sky; nor is it a very good language to explain why 100 people died in the crash. It is a wonderful language to express our sorrow for those who died, comfort those who grieve, and express our joy for those who lived.

Many people are uplifted and inspired with poetic and symbolic expressions, but they've often had to turn off their rational mind and factual knowledge completely to participate in "modern-day" religious worship. That seems both intellectually and theologically dishonest and unnecessary. Upon discovering that many historical religious teachings are based neither on factual nor infallible authorities, some turn their backs on all historical based religious beliefs and expressions. Unfortunately this throws out some meaningful poetry and inspiration too, a language that well addresses our emotional needs. When I came home to my mother's for Christmas and went to church with her after my new religious enlightenment from my seminary studies, I got very frustrated that her local minister continued to limit his preaching to the same old mythologies. So I would criticize the minister and the service when we got home. My mother, who could more than adequately take care of herself in any discussion, pointed out that she really didn't care what my rational mind (and hers) concluded to be factually true. She knew that the worship service was meaningful to her, "so keep your enlightenment out of my faith, and eat your chicken".

She was right, of course. I would never have intruded my own personal feelings or theological views into psychotherapy sessions with my clients and patients. I only did it with my mother because I knew she loved me and would understand my excitement about my new spiritual enlightenment. I was half right. She loved me. But it was also one of those times when we realize that we will have to go on alone when we go beyond the wisdom of our parents and religious leaders to find our own understandings. Even now I fear that the kind of thoughts expressed here will offend some, but I also know there are many others who want to nurture their spiritual nature but struggle to do so within the limitations of traditional religious concepts. Most religious and theological underpinnings in our society end at a child's intellectual level. The same stories and explanations are given to three year-olds in religious teachings as are given to thirty and eighty year-olds. When young people grow up and start to think for themselves, is it any wonder participation in organized religion drops off? Childlike explanations run counter to grownup experience, to what we know and experience about how things really happen—but we still need the personal inspiration, hope, and faith that the stories nurture.

When we look at more scientific explanations of creation, some of the special relationship between God, humans, and creation in religion explanations seems to diminish. Before we get too upset at what appears to be little evidence of a consciously planned creation specially for human beings to live in, however, let us remember and appreciate that some of the best inventions and discoveries have always come from accidental and serendipitous events. Without creation and evolution, there is both Everything, and Nothing, the Completely Perfect, and yet it is all just potential and non-existent. If the Pre-existing All is now continuously evolving and expressing itself in ever-changing forms, we really are a part of that expanding expression of God. God really did create us after all. It just took a very long time. This seems more emotionally comforting than to say our birth was a totally unplanned pregnancy, a mere mistake of cosmic proportions.

All Existence depends on creation. Without creation, nothing but possibility can exist. Without the Big Bang, there is nothing, only the possibility of everything. Without re-creation, what is, cannot continue. The All must create and keep recreating in order to be. Even if everything eventually collapses again into One, it may need to create again in some way in an endless series of Cosmic Big Bangs and Giant Sucking Sounds in order to be. And we, my fellow overly brain-cell-endowed human friends, are part of that evolving expression that has now allowed God to become human, conscious, and caring.

Humans: Co-Creators with God

Why is there human life? Some people have speculated that when everything was One, that it contained ideas as well as all matter and energy. This concept suggests that the idea of a tree and humans beings existed from eternity, long before there ever were any. Eventually after the Big Bang blew bits of matter and energy in all directions, and it cooled for several million years, and galaxies and planets that had atmospheres formed and a billion or so more years went by, eventually a blade of grass and finally, a tree grew. If God had the idea of forming a tree right from the beginning, either the production techniques need a little improvement to get them up to a more useful speed, or God could use a course on time management. The idea that the evolution of humans was an accident, or at least an unplanned event, fits logical speculation as well or better than the idea that God had such a great idea that one day that it blew its mind into a material universe in order to create trees and people after several billion years. Perhaps so. Evolutionary chance is a simpler and seemingly more likely explanation than is an explanation of purposefully delayed creation. Now that God has manifest itself as human beings, however, there is the possibility for even faster and more sophisticated creation.

Coming to understand how gravity works provides an elementary example of how human beings have become Co-Creators. Gravity has been around for a very long time, quietly at work but without a lot of understanding. Our caveman ancestors noticed that if they dropped a big rock, they had better move their toes and that it's not a good idea to sleep under a coconut tree. Our awareness and knowledge of gravity expanded and developed to where we eventually built water towers and roller coasters to make use of this force. Now we even deliberately drop astronauts out of space right back to landing spots on earth and accurately predict the amount that light from a star will bend when passing a galaxy based on our precise knowledge of that gravitational force. We will continue to shape life on Earth by our expanding understanding and knowledge of the nature of Nature. Until the evolution of highly developed instincts and conscious thought, information about the universe and the laws of nature existed but were not observed nor manipulated. We now, however, even have the knowledge and ability to destroy Earth as a place where current life forms could exist. We now have the knowledge and ability to create new life forms through cloning and genetic engineering. We can both create and destroy whole species of life, one possibility perhaps no more awesome and daunting than the other. The development of human consciousness on Earth has here raised God's abilities from chance beginnings to deliberate creation.

Even with our advancing understanding, it seems likely there may always be more information that is unknown than is known, but our increased knowledge increases our ability and responsibility as Co-Creators with God. The forces that keep fingers reproducing as fingers instead of corn stalks on the end of our arms is increasingly known to us. We know the information is contained in the DNA, and it is designed to keep reproducing. It is DNA information that allows us to clone an identical plant and to clone an exact duplicate human being, physically just like the one we are now. We are now faced not just with the ability to create human life in test tubes. We are faced with what we're going to do with all the excess eggs and sperm we collect, and fetuses we create, and what to do when we can create any kind of human being we want, and eventually even beyond human beings. We also can stimulate parts of the brain electrically, magnetically, or chemically and change our mood and perception. Should we make human beings happy all the time? The high spirited debates about human engineering will stir up more moral anguish and debate than abortion and euthanasia ever did. The challenge for ethical direction and consensus for our role as increasingly powerful Co-Creators will not only continue but also deepen.

Rightfully there are fears that some group will use their knowledge to gain an advantage or breed a superior race. When we exercise even more of our ability to select and create human life, traditional religious concepts about the sacredness of human life, based on God having created man, will not be large enough nor strong enough to help with the enormous moral and ethical decisions that these developments present. To argue that creation is sacred and should be left up to God (chance) is a romantic thought, but it's not going to happen. We need a philosophical and spiritual perspective that provides a basis for the ethics of co-creation because when humans have any knowledge and the ability to do something, including engineer human life forms, we use it. Do we really think that some parents or young athletes do not already seek out human growth and strength enhancing hormones to change the athletic ability of God's child? We will use our knowledge! We developed the atomic bomb. We used it! We developed germ warfare. We used it! We developed genetic engineering. We used it! We must find a moral and spiritual stance for guiding our actions that is not based just on God as creator, but is based on humans as Co-Creators with God, hopefully still sacred, respectful and life-embracing, but reaching far beyond traditional religious and theological foundations and teachings.

As our powerful knowledge and abilities to shape our Earth expand, hopefully so will our thoughtfulness, inclusiveness, and humility. In spite of each of us being a material expression of God and co-authors of creation, we are still only like a grain of sugar dropped somewhere in the cosmic river of creation, each identifiable for awhile and then reabsorbed into the ever-flowing current, the sweet impression of our having been, still there; the flow forever, if infinitesimally changed by the addition of our special flavor. The choices we make season not only our own lives but the lives of our children and their children's children and the beings that will exist a billion years from now. For this precious moment, we are part of the developing consciousness of the Universe, Co-creators with God. This life we are given is a small but an incredible divine gift to help shape the next evolution of Creation.

Our Current Creation Myth

15 billion years ago there was a Big Bang. While one can always ask what was before that, our current best answer seems to be both Nothing and Everything Possible. It is the point where everything was more clearly One. That One Thing was not anywhere, but was also everywhere because there was also nothing else. Those who investigate these things debate vigorously whether it was 10 or 20 billion years ago, but really, what difference do a few billion years make to you and me? In less than an instant, one ten billionth of a trillionth of a trillionth of a second something happened. The One blew apart and made a small but quickly expanding concoction of energy and matter. Quarks and electrons formed. Within the first second quarks formed into protons and neutrons. Within the first minute things began to cool down and the first nuclei of hydrogen and helium begin to form. In the next 300,000 years things really cooled off, down to about 3,000 degrees Fahrenheit and photons escaped, and there was light! The first atoms began to form and were collected together. Stars began to spin off in all directions in another 2 billion years, but galaxies didn't begin to form until 5 billion years later. It took 10 billion years for solar systems and planets such as Earth to form. The last 4 billion years or so our sun and galaxy have just been calming down a bit as the universe continues its now more quiet expansion. Only a few million years ago life forms began to emerge on Earth. (Robert S. Boyd. Knight-Ridder Newspapers. 1/21/96).

And, yes, lest we be totally overlooked, the common ancestor of apes and humans seems to have started developing about 5-7 million years ago. Apparently after a few sub-species tried but died off, the first Homo Sapiens finally evolved only about 100,000 year ago. The prominence of human life in this process can be illustrated by thinking of this evolution in compressed time. If all time since the Big Bang were compressed into 4 years, human beings have been around only for the last 13 minutes. To speculate that humans might be among the higher life forms in the Universe is by no means certain and it seems quite likely that the evolutionary process could have proceeded at greater speed or in a different direction elsewhere in the universe. Our sun is estimated to be one of 50 to 100 million in our medium sized galaxy called the Milky Way, which is one of about 50 billion galaxies in the universe. Calculating these possibilities, with 5,000,000,000,000,000,000 suns and innumerable planets orbiting around them, it becomes inconceivable to believe that there is intelligent life only on Earth.

Just as there came a time when we had to adjust our theological and philosophical perspectives to the idea that the Earth was not the center of the universe, it appears that we now have to adjust both to the idea that humans may not be the most developed life form in the universe and that human like consciousness was probably not around before our evolution. While human beings are a very curious and wonderful development, there is no evidence that they are a central or necessary part of creation. We resist incorporating this thought into our religious and theological thinking because we're frightened that if we are not the central purpose of creation, we might not be important at all. Theology and religions have provided the reassuring thought that some human like person must have made all this and is directing the show, with us specially in mind, of course. Some religions further suggest that if we live right, we'll get another life bestowed on us from this cosmic personality, so we don't have to worry quite so much about the deficiencies of this one. Others religions have solved the deficiencies and struggles of our existence by saying that what we perceive as real in this life is only temporary or illusionary and the really important stuff of existence is waiting for us in some other realm so, again, we need not get too upset about our current, very mortal and finite fears.

Sometimes people act irrationally certain in the face of their possible limited significance, shouting their beliefs defiantly into the fearful abyss. Some calm their fears by vehemently proclaiming that their particular explanation of life's origin and meaning is actually the only correct one—and all non-believers are the only ones who have anything to fear. Their need to prove they are right leads to judging, shunning, persecuting, firing, estranging, or even killing people who don't agree. We still experience one ethnic or religious group actually trying to exterminate another. Those who feel insulted by a deviant interpretation of their religious texts have sometimes declared some form of holy vendetta and try to kill those who speak with a different thoughtfulness. We see those who proclaim the sacredness of life and are against those who believe in abortion, kill those who perform or seek them. Human beings are a pretty amazing product of evolution, but they clearly need some more work! We have not been around so long, and we have certainly not yet distinguished ourselves well enough to have earned the self aggrandizing claim to be God's only spokespersons. Ninety percent of the matter in the universe is not even visible to humans, possibly even containing existence unlike what we know. Not only are human beings a minority of the material creation of the earth, galaxy, and universe, but that part of the material universe in which we live is a small minority of all that exists. So we better humble-up a bit when it comes to claiming that our particular understanding of creation, its purpose, and its meaning should be universally accepted and religiously revered.

Emotionally, however, we need help! We desire to be reassured of our place or importance in some way in order to deal with the basic fearful aloneness that accompanies our separation/birth into individual existence. On an intellectual level we are also curious and want to understand how this creation stuff works. We inevitably use human-like metaphors to address our needs and questions. When faced with all this vastness and wonder, "What created all this?" is as logical a question as "Who created all this?" It is more emotionally satisfying, however, to personalize this contemplation. In the past this has only widened the gap between our emotional and intellectual understanding, but we can continue to bring our emotional and intellectual understanding closer together if we are not afraid to accept that we have conceptualized God with a personality in our own image.

The personification of God is similar to the philosophical conundrum: "If a tree falls in the forest and there is no one around to hear it fall, is there any sound?" One answer is, there is no sound unless someone is there to perceive it. There are vibrational waves that are sent through the ground and air when the tree falls, but unless these waves encounter something that interprets it, there is no sound. How would a beetle interpret a falling tree? With some vibrational message of generic danger? Or maybe it is a stimulant to eat: "Oh, good, lunch in a few months. I better inch right on over there!" When a tree falls, there is the creation of vibration, which when it runs into a human ear causes the ear drum to vibrate, which communicates to the brain, where it is combined with visual information (Look, there is a tree moving sideways!) to conclude: This is the sound of a tree falling! Until it is perceived, vibrational waves are only the potential for sound. When it is perceived and interpreted, however, it expands into a new form of meaning. So it is with our conception of God. When we humans perceive our personal connection to the Source Of Everything and our place in the creation process, we bring the evolution of Creation into a new level of meaning and God into a more sophisticated, personally human level of self awareness.

Our connection to the God that is Everything has no inherent purpose beyond simple existence and the continuation of the life of our species until we become aware of our connection and assign it meaning, like a vibrational wave awaiting interpretation. Until there is human perception, God is just the matter and energy of existence, like the tree falling in the forest with no one around to hear it. It takes a human mind with some form of knowledge, reflection, sensitivity, and experience to change vibration into meaningful sound and the awareness of a source of all creation into a personal awareness of God. God did not exist in the same form before human consciousness perceived it; and when we encounter this connection in our own awareness, the kind of God we encounter is shaped by our own ability to perceive, our personality, what we were taught to believe, and by our experience.

Our modern world has brought us to a point of renewed spiritual interest as well as increased knowledge of both the physical and non-material universe. It is a perfect time for creating newer, more modern metaphors of meaning. It is honest to recognize that worshipping a Father/Mother god is a filtered expression of our emotional need for reassurance in the vastness of the universe rather than as a scientific explanation that some gigantic man/woman sat down at a work bench and tinkered together some planets, suns and other cosmic stuff for us. This recognition that we rational perceivers of the laws of nature are also emotional beings who often need to experience our connection to the Universe in personal terms is not a philosophical inconsistency. It allows for a more complete integration of our human nature than religious philosophy that requires intellectual impossibility or the denial of human emotion in our spiritual formulations. Nor does it require the idea that the human body is only an illusionary or meaningless vessel in which the more important part of existence, the soul or spirit, is temporarily housed. That is not how we experience ourselves nor encounter reality. We experience things as very physical <u>and</u> very emotional and to offer spiritual understanding that separates or does not fully integrate both is incomplete or just reassuringly dishonest.

Much of the interpretation and understanding of spiritual awareness that our ancestors and historical based religions have used to explain creation and the place of human beings in the universe are so at odds with what we know intellectually and scientifically today that our past concepts and perception of God must inevitably be updated or discarded. When we hear what the astronomers and physicists are telling us about the nature of creation and the universe, it sounds no less incredible, no less astounding, and certainly more awesome to comprehend than simpler more ancient mythologies. At the same time we can also expect that our newer understandings of creation will be superseded by further understanding and interpretation that will probably make our current creation myths also seem simplistic and outdated.

The Human Limits of Knowledge

Hang on, dear reader. This is going to get pretty wild, but it will only last a few pages and then we can all go back to thinking we're under control. Three hundred years ago Isaac Newton began to outline some of the laws of physics that describe the underlying principles of matter and creation. We learned to predict how far a baseball will go when hit with a bat swung at a certain speed or when to launch a rocket so it will rendezvous with a satellite that is orbiting the earth.

Now we are predicting and discovering what happens at the level of atoms and subatomic particles. We can now understand and predict actions at subatomic levels of creation so small and short-lived that we have never seen any of it, only the remains.

Newton's predecessor, Galileo, was imprisoned by the Roman Catholic Church for suggesting that the earth revolved around the sun. Descartes subsequently fashioned a compromise with the Church where science, which was based on investigation and experimentation that anyone could repeat, would deal only with the material world; spiritual and psychological knowledge would be dealt with only by the Church. This later allowed Newton and others to push ahead our understanding of the physical world with the endorsement of the scientific method, but our understanding and development of our spiritual and emotional nature remained deliberately restrained with pre-17th century thinking. The intellectual separation of our material nature from our spiritual and emotional natures has artificially divided up the mental, physical, and spiritual understanding of our being human, making each of these perspectives less than whole. Ironically it is the new physicists, not religious or spiritual thinkers, who provide new spiritual understanding and the strongest impetus for bringing science, psychology, and spirituality back together.

Just when we thought we had the rules of creation about figured out enough that we could predict and determine the outcome of most everything, we discovered that at a sub-atomic level, we can only predict the probability of occurrences. The most distinguishing characteristic of quantum physics is that it challenges our expectation, our everyday experience, and common sense. It is simply incredible and astounding! In quantum physics we find out that at the smallest and most basic level of material existence, we cannot predict what will happen like Newtonian science led us to expect. Every time the same factors are introduced together, we should get the same result. Every time a baseball with the same composition is hit with the same force, with the same bat, at the same angle, we should be able to predict where the ball will land—figuring for the wind, of course. But at the subatomic level of events we can only predict the probability of something happening:

> Suppose that we put one gram of radium in a time vault and leave it there for sixteen hundred years. When we return, do we find one gram of radium? No! We find only half a gram. This is because radium atoms naturally disintegrate at a rate such that every sixteen hundred years half of them are gone. Therefore, physicists say that radium has a "half life" of sixteen hundred years. If we put the radium back in the vault for another sixteen hundred years, only one fourth of the original gram would remain when we opened the vault again. Every sixteen hundred years one half of all the radium atoms in the world disappear. How do we know which radium atoms are going to disintegrate and which radium atoms are not going to disintegrate? We don't. We can predict how many atoms in a piece of radium are going to disintegrate in the next hour, but we have no

> way of determining which ones are going to disintegrate. There is no physical law that we know of which governs this selection. Which atoms decay is purely a matter of chance.
> (Gary Zukav: The Dancing Wu Li Masters upon which I am very dependent for the following discussion. The reader is encouraged to read this and other explanations of quantum physics for further understanding of these astonishing interactions of the ultimate stuff.)

Out of any ten atoms of radium we know for sure that half of them, five of them, won't be there in sixteen hundred years. But there is only a fifty-fifty chance that the specific one we bet on to survive, will actually be there or disappear. It doesn't matter which one we pick. The overall outcome is totally predictable. The specific outcome is only posssible.

Our mechanistic view of the universe works well to explain most things, until we get to things like subatomic particles and the speed of light. We then learn that not only energy and mass are properties of the same thing, but also that human consciousness and reality are also properties of the same thing. In fact quantum physicists place such a high role on human consciousness, that things such as space and time and properties of light, exist partially only because we humans perceive, contemplate, think and measure in those terms. The very existence of things partially take their shape when our minds apprehend them. We just had it backwards. Creation did not start with a human-like conscious intention. Human consciousness came into being because of creation and now helps understand its own nature.

The scientific evidence that human consciousness is co-creating reality can be illustrated by studies of the nature of light. We can prove that light is made up of a series of atomic particles that we can direct toward something, such as a piece of metal, and then measure electrons being knocked loose and spinning off. The light particles strike the metal, causing subatomic particles in the metal to be dislodged and fly off, clearly demonstrating light is a stream of particles.

But we can also prove that light is an energy wave, not a particle. If we project a light through a small slit in a piece of paper it will make a soft roundish spot on the wall behind it. If we open an adjacent small slit in the piece of paper and project light through both holes onto the same wall, the roundish spot does not get brighter as we might expect if more particles of light were being added together. Instead a series of lighter and darker bands appear on the wall—a phenomena well known when waves interact with each other. When waves are combined, the peaks get higher and the troughs get lower. When the peaks and troughs of two waves overlap, they cancel each other out. This creates flatness in water or dark lines in a light pattern. So these lighter and darker lines on our wall clearly show that light is an energy wave.

We can show that light clearly acts like a particle and like an energy wave, which should not be possible. It should be one or the other, but it gets even more mind-boggling! If we send only one photon of light through the first slit in the paper, we can detect where it will land on our wall, just like shooting a bullet through the slit and seeing where it strikes the wall. We can mark that landing spot on our wall where it hits with a marker. But when we uncover the other slit in our paper, we discover that our first mark on the wall is in an area which is now dark when both slits are open. That is, our first photon of light hit the wall where there is no light when the second slit is open. So how does the photon in the first try "know" that it can land in an area where it never goes when the second slit is open? What determines where the first photon goes, rests on what is happening at the other slit, whether it is open or closed. But how does our photon going through the first slit, know whether the second hole is open or closed and therefore know where it can and cannot go?

The choices to explain this phenomenon reflect different assumptions about the nature of reality:

1. The knowledge of whether the second slit is open or closed is transferred to the first photon at a speed of light or greater, or independent of light speed. This interpretation is favored by those who want to demonstrate that there is a spiritual or non-material, non-localized nature to reality.
2. The electron valences cancel each other and it only appears that the direction of the light was changed. (Victor Stenger: "Quantum Quackery". The Skeptical Inquirer, Vol. 21, No. 1, January/February 1997.) This interpretation is favored by those who want to demonstrate that the ultimate reality is basically materialistic and mechanical.

3. The outcome is determined by what the perceiver/believer chooses to measure. This interpretation is favored by those who emphasize the importance of consciousness in creating reality.

Each of these interpretations seems to be possible but this fact in itself helps support the third argument that it is our human consciousness that is critical to creating the nature of reality. Not until we attempt to measure it, does the photon go one place or the other, act more like a particle or a wave. Not until then does the nature of light take on this specific reality. Until then both things are possible and true. When we measure or observe it, only one thing is possible, just as it is possible to measure for certain only the position or the momentum of a sub-atomic particle. Human consciousness is the co-creator of this ultimate reality. Without conscious perception, there is something, potential or form at another level of existence, but light, just like theology, ethics and moral behavior, does not have final form until we humans shape it by our perception, understanding, and choices. Newtonian science suggested that the key to understanding is measuring what is out there, but we now know that human consciousness shapes the reality of what is out there. There was only a predictable probability of where the photon would land until it was measured. After we measured it, there is a 100% chance of where it landed and the other possibility is zero. When human consciousness observes or becomes aware of something, not only does it take on new meaning but in some cases its potential becomes a new form of reality. Not until humans perceive it does God take on human-like characteristics.

Even after accepting that human consciousness helps determine the nature of reality, we then have to further admit that our own perceptions and measurements are not constant, but have a variable reality of their own. To illustrate this scientists ask us to think about measuring how long it takes for something to happen. Think about two trains with those big headlights on them pointed toward each other, one in the station in Anderson and the other in the station at Butler, exactly 100 miles apart. If one train in Anderson heads towards Butler at 50 miles an hour, it will take two hours for the headlights on the two trains to pass each other if the Butler train remains unmoving in the station. If the trains are both heading toward each other at a speed of 50 miles an hour each, however, they approach each other at a combined speed of 100 mph and it would only take one hour for them to pass each other.

If we accelerate our trains to the speed of light, however, something strange happens to our measurement of time and speed. Suppose we put our train headlight on an object in a neighboring galaxy and boost up its power, let's say to the power of a star shining in that galaxy. We then measure how long it takes for the light from that sun to reach us at the speed of light that travels at 186,00 miles per second. But the galaxies are also moving in relation to each other. If our sun and galaxy were moving toward the other sun and galaxy at 10,000 miles per second (mps), we would expect that the relative speed of the light approaching us from the other galaxy would be

196,000 mps; but it's not! It's still only 186,000 mps! If we were to measure another star that was moving away from us at 10,000 miles per second, the light from that cousin star would still reaches us at the rate of 186,000 mps, not at 176,000 mps. Where does the extra 10,000 miles per second go? You wouldn't think something that big could be easily misplaced! What happens is that time adjusts for space. Oh please, don't tell me this! Clocks run slower and faster. Yardsticks expand and contract when we're on a cosmic scale. Sooner, Later, and Now are only relative terms for our conscious organization and convenience.

The non-absolute nature of time seems particularly weird until we remember from our experience in dreams or other altered states of consciousness that we are quite capable of perceiving reality without "normal" time and space. It's just that when we are awake, we think our perception of time is more "real". So our consciousness helps organize a reality that is limited, not just because we cannot comprehend the mysteries and magnitude of creation any other way but also in order to make things more mentally manageable. Our consciousness helps us organize, know, think, and comprehend what would otherwise be unmanageable knowledge or chaos.

For Quark Hunters, a Minute Surprise

> In 1964, in one of the great conceptual leaps of modern science, physicist Murray Gell-Mann and George Zweig asserted that six fundamental entities, which they called "quarks" make up

> most of the substance of matter. Having proved this on paper, they turned it over to experimental physicists to verify—a process that was completed ... at the Fermi National Accelerator Laboratory in Batavia, Ill.
> The experiments at Fermilab began to yield results that called into question the essence of the quark, which is its indivisibility. Quarks are never observed directly, only deduced by observing collisions between protons and antiprotons in a particle accelerator. According to a paper...certain results suggested that quarks may actually be composed of even smaller and more fundamental particles. If true...this raises the disturbing possibility that the universe will never surrender its ultimate material, that beneath every level of particles lurks another, still more esoteric·and inaccessible. (Newsweek: February 19, 1996)

If we take our heads out of our accelerators, we may conclude that it is probably the way our minds can conceive of the questions that are contributing to the outcome of our search for the ultimate particle of existence. Before the most minute particle what is there? We will always keep asking these mechanistic questions of curiosity because it reflects how we organize and understand knowledge. We have attempted to answer this question by studying matter. We may always find some smaller bit of existence because of the way we keep asking the question. We discovered when determining that light acts both like waves and particles, that it is the question we ask and what we choose to measure that helps determine the nature of ultimate reality. If we ask whether the ultimate nature of reality is not matter at all but rather energy or information, the answer to that question may also be "Yes, that too!"

Beyond Reality to Significance

Searching for the ultimate minute material or energy of creation is still only trying to address the question of "how" things work. It doesn't attempt to answer the question of "why". When we realize that the answer to both the how and the why questions about creation are shaped by our own human consciousness, we have started to reintegrate science, psychology, and spirituality. The answer to how and why we exist will always be greatly shaped by our consciousness and our emotions because that is from where the question arises. Our consciousness shapes our understanding and the nature of reality. Together with our emotions they determines our perception of reality and what is ultimately important. Each of us will answer with our life choices, decisions, and commitments why we are here and how we interpret the importance of our connection to the Unifying Force of the Universe. Ultimately, we answer cosmic "Why" questions by how we live out the gift of our lives. Not just prophets, not just Mohammed or Moses or Buddha or Jesus or Confucius, but each of us is the revelation and expression of God's presence and consciousness on Earth.

In the beginning there was the potential for everything, but it was also nothing for there was no expression, no being, no consciousness, no existence. And we call it God, Allah, or something else Great. And then God became expressed in information and knowledge and material form, and light and energy, and eventually human conscious awareness. And God took the form of things totally invisible, but also of galaxies and stars and planets and air and water and plants and animals and you and me. And sometimes we become aware that it is still all God, and each of us, individually is an expression of God. And we are awed, and acknowledge our source, and feel we belong, and know everything is ultimately and infinitely all right. And there is joy and dancing and singing right here in this little speck of the Universe we call Earth as we little ones celebrate belonging to God. And God is celebrating too, for just as we have evolved from God, God has evolved with us.

Miracles

Endless Possibilities

Right Before Our Eyes

This chapter could have been a one-liner: "There aren't any."

But that doesn't fully describe our experience. By definition, if anything happens, it is part of the Natural Order. Just because we don't know how something came about, does not mean there was a breaking of the laws of the universe or nature. It just means we don't understand all the possibilities of what can happen. There are some unexplainable, awe-inspiring, wonderful events that cause us to appreciate and celebrate how surprising and wondrous life can be; and it is appropriate to express our excitement and surprise by exclaiming that it is miraculous. This is a long way, however, from showing any evidence that a cosmic exception occurred on our behalf to win the lottery, recover from cancer, or survive a building collapse in a hurricane. It makes no more sense to attribute these "miracles" to special divine intervention than it does to blame God for our not winning the lottery, dying from cancer, or a building collapse that killed our loved ones.

We have an emotional urge to celebrate and express our undeserved good fortune. A "miracle" is a proclamation of joy, surprise, gratitude and awe. It is not a factual explanation of why something happened. When we're feeling especially lucky or blessed, nobody gives a hoot about "Why" anyway. Thank you, Jesus! Praise

God! Allah is Mighty! Let's eat and drink and give thanks! "Miracle" is our joyful designation of things we didn't expect, don't particularly deserve, and can't explain. When a player catches a football that bounces off the hands of two other people in the last second for a come from behind Super Bowl victory, it seems a bit understated to suggest it is just the logical consequences of the laws of physics. For those people who were out riding their bikes, cleaning up the house, or caring for a sick loved one and didn't care to watch the BIG GAME, the recitation of the laws of physics are appropriately boring to describe how the ball ended up in the receiver's hands. For them this could never be a miracle. For the individual player, their family, fans, and bookies in Las Vegas, this can be a miraculous, joyful, unexpected, and undeserved cause for celebration.

Usually we reserve our most solemn declarations of miracles to the continuation of a life when it was endangered, such as the plane crash that killed 167 people but left one alive. Now the fact that one survives is pretty amazing, not satisfyingly expressed by the laws of physics that can describe exactly what happened. We don't tend to call it miraculous, however, when the sun comes up every morning. Now that's pretty wonderful, but we expected it; so we let our mechanical explanations describe it. We also don't call it a miracle if we walk out the door and there's live shark in our driveway. That's pretty exciting, unexpected, and not easily explained; but we wouldn't call it a miracle. We want to know who's the idiot with the weird sense of humor. Miracles are joyful surprises that make us appreciate being alive. "It's a miracle" is another way of saying, "I feel great to be alive right now!"

Before I concluded that hitting myself with a hammer would be more enjoyable, I used to ask my pre-adolescent son a friendly "How was your day?" He often responded with signs of severe hearing loss. Since my own parents had my hearing tested without success for a similar disease when I was young, I reluctantly concluded that watching the first 30 seconds of a TV rerun was more important than saying "Hello" to his incredibly wonderful, loving father. I was helped to this conclusion when his silences were sometimes interspersed with an occasional "Go away!" This event was always unexpected, unexplainable, and undeserved, but the only miraculous thing about it was that I didn't strangle him on the spot. What strikes us as miraculous always includes a good feeling. It is our mental interpretation and emotional state that transforms natural events into the miraculous. If you told me that the neighbor of a cousin of a great aunt of yours was dying of cancer and then unexpectedly went into remission and recovered, it has little more personal impact than telling me that hams are on sale at the supermarket. If I'm busy planning a dinner for guests or have my own loved one dying, I'll probably ask you for more details. Otherwise I'll probably politely nod my head and say, "Oh, that's interesting". We confine the word "miracle" to things that make us happy and appreciative.

The ability of medical science to transplant and clone human cells is going to produce amazing possibilities that will equal what Nature has created so far. Human beings will increasingly direct previously unheard of and astounding physical regeneration. We probably won't consider them miracles because we understand them, and because of that we lose some of our awe; but we should not let that happen. We can create more and more miracles if we are careful. If we do not treat our abilities as Co-Creators with reverence and responsibility, we will create not miracles, but plagues of biblical proportions and the only miracle will be whether the human race keeps from destroying itself. It would be nice to see how good we humanoids could get at miracle making in another couple of million years.

For now, religious and non-religious pilgrims travel the world over to sites rumored to have brought miraculous healing to others. The shrine at Lourdes is perhaps the most well known and publicized for producing unexpected healings. Occasionally, something unexplained, and wonderful happens there. A young girl, later to be designated Saint Bernadette by the Roman Catholic Church, had a vision of the Virgin Mary at Lourdes in 1858. Because the Church does not want ridicule or false claims about miraculous healings, they carefully scrutinize these claims. Out of the hundred of thousands who have gone there, less than a hundred miracles have been endorsed and certified by the Catholic Church. It is indeed amazing and wonderful that people with diseases incurable by other attempts occasionally get better from these pilgrimages.

I visited a similar site at the Sanctuario de Chimayo in New Mexico. Off the main chapel there is a small adobe room hung with crutches, pictures, written testimonials, and lighted candles of praise and thanksgiving from those who have felt some form of healing during their visit to the shrine. Some of these visitors apparently have experienced wonderful, unexplained changes in their physical or emotional functioning. Over the years many people have commented on the irony of these shrines. While some people discard their wheel chairs and crutches, no one leaves wooden legs or glass eyes. Clearly spiritually initiated healing doesn't work all the time and in fact has clear limitations. Even with our most focused and fervent hopes and beliefs and unexplained good fortune, we can't yet replace missing body parts, get a facelift, keep from ever getting sick, or bring back the dead. So even the realm of "miraculous healing" is limited to the known and unknown laws of nature. For an adult human being to suddenly or even gradually grow a new leg or eyeball where previously there wasn't one is beyond our regenerative abilities or that of current medical science. Some day we'll be able to make these things happen and hopefully we'll still remember to appreciate the wonder even after we understand how to do it. It is unfortunate and shameful that some evangelists have taken the occasional miraculous joy of spontaneous unexplained healing and turned it into a self-promotional money-scam scheme. There is clearly healing power in hope and belief as well as in medical knowledge, but both should be honored with grateful awe without desecrating the gift.

The fact that the human body can heal itself or that other physical occurrences can be influenced by human conscious and unconscious thought is an expression of natural law, not a breaking of it. These events appear unexpectedly to us because with the advent of scientific methodology, we mistakenly removed unconscious knowledge, emotion, and spirit from our expectations of what influences material events. Human beings regularly survive germs and environmental attacks for 70 or 80 years, even if they never see a doctor. It is obvious that more people make it that far if they take advantage of medical knowledge and skills, but the basic healing mechanisms are built in at birth. It is perfectly normal that human bodies try to stay alive and repair themselves. It's when we can't figure out how something works that we proclaim it miraculous. For those who had never seen it or had any understanding, television, antibiotics, and automobiles would all be miracles; but they are really wonderful outgrowths of our expanding understanding and application of the laws of nature. That which becomes common place tends to no longer be a source of joy or awe for us. We even get angry when our cars won't start or the electricity goes off! Hopefully we can remember the things in our lives that were once miraculous and remain grateful.

Our own attitude is the most fertile place from which the miraculous can emerge. It is from our own appreciation and awareness that we will encounter the recurring miraculous events around us. Miracles are emotional and spiritual joys available to those who look for them. They are everywhere we appreciate and celebrate life.

> Ordinary miracles happen all around…
> Ev'ry sun that rises, never rose before.
> Each new day leads the way
> Through a diff'rent door….

Ordinary miracles, one for ev'ry star
No light'ning bolt or clap of thunder
Only joy and quiet wonder.
Endless possibilities right before our eyes....

("Ordinary Miracles". Words by Alan &
Marilyn Bergman. Music by Marvin Hamlisch.
Threesome Music Co. & Red Bullet Music.
Polygram International Publishing, 1994.)

Prayer and Other Timeless Pursuits

May we feel the Spirit around us.
May we experience our spirit within.
May we know our spirits are One.

Prayer is a purposeful changing of the usual focus of our attention. Prayer-states include diverse forms of altered consciousness experienced in quiet mediation, religious incantations, communal ritual, dance and rhythmic movement, deep states of relaxation, imagery, hypnosis, energy work, internal self talk, yoga, music, and others. We are always surrounded by and contain knowledge beyond our conscious awareness, but we have to refocus our minds and bodies in order for us to become more aware of the alignment of our individual existence with the larger existence of the Universe. Prayer does not have to be in a particular (religious) format. We don't have to be a "good person", good Buddhist, Christian, or Muslim or even a believer in prayer for us to engage in some for of it. If communicating with the Ground of our Being requires a particular religious format, then we would have to engage in the futile discussion whether Baptist prayer is better than Presbyterian, or Pentecostal prayer is worse than Roman Catholic, or whether Hindu prayers are more effective than Taoist ones. To contend that a particular religious interpretation of any of our spirituality is the only correct one, is reassuring to the individual proclaiming it, but hardly promotes the fellowship of man nor the expression of a universal source of our existence. Some of the most arrogant and self righteous statements come from religious and secular devotees who assert that anyone who does not believe as they do is doomed to eternal damnation or should be ostracized. This narrow minded, holier-than-thou, self-justification sometimes leads to cruelty ranging from religious and political wars to assertions that if this person hadn't sinned, had practiced a better prayer life, or had believed more faithfully they wouldn't have gotten sick, lost their child, or had their house burn down.

The Dimensions of Prayer

Prayer is a universal human experience of altered consciousness with a multitude of forms, all of them capable of calming our fears and strengthening our spirit. The fact is that we can nourish our spirits independent of any religious beliefs at all, and there are many more secular forms of prayer than religious ones. If we commune with Nature on a walk, engage in meditation or use deep breathing or alpha wave biofeedback to quiet and calm ourselves, we are communicating with a part of our unconscious and a part of the Universe to which we do not normally attend. If we use mental imagery to help encourage healing in our body, we are using a form of prayer, communicating with the Spirit of Re-Creation that is within and around us. Bowing our heads and closing our eyes is a traditional ritual of prayer, but prayer states are also entered through chanting, by taking a deep breath and letting go of all conscious thoughts, as well as through singing, rhythms, and the "talking to ourselves" or to God that many people do under their breath or in their thoughts. The line between religious forms of prayer and secular ones are as permeable as the lines between what is spiritual, emotional, and physical.

Because the mind, body, and spirit are inseparable manifestations of the same being, prayer that helps us be aware of our connection to the Spirit of everything, can be initiated from any part of our being. The more formal traditional prayers of church services connect us to our ancestors who also had awareness of their spirituality. Music that stirs deep within us and reaches beyond the words being sung connects us to the emotion and energy of the Life-Spirit. Popular music can stir the soul and express in words the celebration of our spirituality as well, or sometimes better, than the traditional music of our temples. Quiet meditation and silence can bring the comfort and awareness of peace and belonging. The peacefulness one feels during yoga or Chi Qong is the equivalent of the peacefulness of "turning to God in prayer". These are all forms of prayer, all experiences of letting go of our normal way of thinking and concentrating, letting the thinking part of our brains relax and letting other portions of awareness become more active. The result is that we focus on another part of our existence, an awareness that reaches beyond our usual consciousness and beyond our own individuality.

If we don't expand our understanding and concept of prayer to include other experiences beyond traditional worship forms, we overlook just how spiritual many people are who are not formally religious and do not necessarily direct their prayer to a god. Traditionally prayers were directed somewhere, usually up, perhaps because this was where Heaven might be located and God presumably would be in the same general vicinity. (In an almost infinite universe, exactly what direction is up?) But people also offer prayers to Mother Earth, or in order to "ground" themselves emotionally. Sending prayer outward in all direction at the same time, inward through ourselves, or merging our consciousness with the Ground of Our Being is all the same.

It does not matter the direction we conceive prayer to go, but the choice to conceive of prayer as directed toward an external point, an internal point, or a non-point depends a lot on the dominant religious/cultural view in which we are raised. Those who emphasize the presence of the spiritual without direction are following not only the example of Christian mystics, but also of Eastern religious traditions which encourage the experience of the highest levels of spiritual awareness through repressing external awareness and focusing just on consciousness itself. Because European and American culture has usually conceived of God and prayer to be externally focused, internally focused prayer or meditation without being sent to a place or direction has been less practiced.

Epithets of "Go to Hell" do not raise the issue of location because they are not seen as references to real places. They are interpreted as the angry, rude and boorish behavior they are meant to be. We hear this language freely today not only because Hell has lost power as a concept and we are more socially undisciplined and impolite, but also because most people have stopped thinking of Hell as a real place. We tend to talk about hell on earth, inner torture, mental turmoil and inner torment of the soul rather than a future experience. Not only have most people stopped using the Devil myth, we also have almost stopped using the Hell myth because we increasingly conceive of spiritualty as a non-local state of consciousness. “The Devil made me do it” isn’t as humorous as it used to be because it’s been a long time since most of us believed that our world is affected by invisible personalities. It’s funnier to say the herbal tea made me do it, or the Twinkies, because most of us, including defense lawyers and psycho-babble cultists, currently assign more power to Twinkies than to the Devil. We look for explanation for events more internally and increasingly assign more responsibility to individual consciousness and emotion than to external forces.

Similarly we will probably increasingly internalize our conception of how and where we contact God, because it fits better with our emotional experience. It also fits well with our intellectual knowledge from physics and brain research that shows that our own consciousness helps determine both material reality and our spiritual perceptions. We are most commonly aware of the presence of God in internal feelings of peacefulness and calmness. The experience and feeling of being linked infinitely to the All without time and space starts from within our brain. It is an experience that can be triggered by meditation or prayer, but it is an experience that has also repeatedly been induced by electrically or electromagnetically stimulating the temporal lobes of the brain.

So prayer doesn’t go anywhere. It is outside time and space, springing forth from our own mind, connecting with things within and beyond our body. This underlying connectedness of everything is always present, always available to our awareness, whether we are interpreting it spiritually or not. Since God is the total material, information, and energy of the Universe and our intentional focus the conscious link, God really does know our prayers before we utter them. God knows what we are going to pray for before we pray it because God is also already in us, our physical being already knowing it's needs and unconscious emotional needs before we are aware of them, the Spirit of Creation and Re-Creation already at work within us before we know to ask it for help. Consciously directed prayer is simply our attempt to boldly suggest to the Universe how our lives or those of other's should proceed. Perhaps this is a tad bit presumptuous given our limited abilities and understanding of the workings of the Universe, but it is a calming and comforting experience in the midst of turmoil and distress.

If, however, we pray to have the laws of nature and physics suspended ("I'd like all balls to fly upwards toward the sun every time they bounce off the ground"), we won't have a good success rate and be reminded of the limitations of prayer. If we pray for a sense of calm and peace and strength to face our problems, we can feel supported by the Infinite Within, even if we can't control it. One of the most fascinating arenas of exploration to us as human beings still remains whether we can at least influence a little bit the material world through our conscious thought, prayer, or mental telepathy. In other words can we change material objects, human bodies, and every day events through any of the many forms of prayer? We understand scientifically now how thoughts, through release of chemicals in the brain and elsewhere, change the physiology of our body. This is also to say that we now understand scientifically how our prayers, emotions, and mental imagery can influence the health of our own bodies. That fact that we can affect our bodies through mental concentration only to a limited degree is perhaps somewhat disappointing, but if we are alone, dying or desperate with no other options, various forms of prayer and mental meditations are as welcome as shark repellent in the ocean at dinner time. Even more intriguing and awe-inspiring than influencing the health of our own bodies, however, is the possibility that our thoughts and prayers might be able to affect the physiology of someone else.

A study by Dr. Randolph Byrd at San Francisco General Hospital seemed to show that praying for patients can produce better healing after heart surgery. These 392 patients were randomly assigned to a group who were prayed for and a group who were not. Neither the patients, doctors, nor nurses knew who was being prayed for and who was not. Fewer patients who were prayed for required antibiotics or the assistance of a mechanical breathing machine, and fewer experienced pulmonary edema. There were also fewer deaths in the prayed for group, and while this was not shown to be statistically significant, it was obviously pretty significant to those who lived. Other studies are now under way to try to verify whether these kinds of findings can be duplicated. Researchers are also curious to find out whether praying for someone else to get well changes their body with an outside force or intervention, or whether it helps the ill person focus their own internal healing resources.

In Byrd's study it was claimed that neither the patients nor staff knew which patients were being prayed for, raising the possibility that it was an outside intervention that had an impact. But even asking whether the healing power of prayer comes from the outside or the inside injects the same mistake on a spiritual level that the church and science made when they asked whether the cause/cure of a disease is mental or physical. Just as the body, mind, and spirit are inseparable expressions of the same thing, the spirit that is present in us is the same Spirit from which everything comes and is outside us. We can artificially separate these experiences for purposes of discussion, but there is no separaton in reality. We do not pray to something outside us that is not also in us and in everything that is. Prayer is communication with ourselves and with the Spirit of All Creation at the same time because it is all part of the same Oneness of Existence. The anatomy of our brain leads us to perceive that we are individual and separate, as minds separate from bodies, as spirits separate from the Spirit, as creation separate from That Which Creates Everything.

Larry Dossey in Healing Words expands the argument that prayer "works" because we have "soul", a shared quality of the Divine.

> Prayer is a genuinely nonlocal event—that is, it is not confined to a specific place in space or to a specific moment in time. Prayer reaches outside the here-and-now; it operates at a

> distance and outside the present moment. Since prayer is initiated by a mental action, this implies that there is some aspect of our psyche that also is genuinely nonlocal. If so, then something of ourselves is infinite in space and time—thus omnipresent, eternal, and immortal. "Nonlocal," after all, does not mean "really big" or "a very long time." It implies infinitude in space and time, because a limited nonlocality is a contradiction in terms. In the West this infinite aspect of the psyche has been referred to as the soul. Empirical evidence for prayer's power, then, is indirect evidence for the soul. It is also evidence for shared qualities with the Divine—"the Divine within"—since infinitude, omnipresence, and eternality are qualities that we have attributed also to the Absolute.

Dossey's statement that because prayer is initiated by human mental action and can transcend space and time perhaps overreaches to suggest that we are, therefore, also non-local, infinite, and immortal beings. Just because human consciousness can think and express without time and space parameters does not prove that our personality or consciousness would exist without our body, nor that our personalities will continue after our body dies. We regularly think without time or space confinements. We do this in our dreams, hypnosis, meditational states, and in our emotions such as our feeling for a loved one—whether they are alive or dead; but that doesn't make us immortal. Dossey also cites the Spendrift prayer research to show that general prayer for God's will to be done has as much effect on the outcome of events, such as the speed of plant growth, as does prayer for a specific outcome. If our consciousness has any effect on physical events, it appears that we have very limited influence and that we do better to try to align ourselves for reassurance with a power greater than ourselves than to try to direct it.

For What Can We Reasonably Pray?

When something happens that we cannot explain, we tend to refer to it as miraculous and be excited, or say our prayers were answered, but in reality most of us don't base our lives on hoping for exceptions to the rules any more than we count on winning the lottery. No matter how hard we pray, it won't produce a new car, win a football game, get a raise, or win the lottery, though according to a popular poll 73% of Americans say they believe they can get a job through prayer. ("Is God Listening?" Newsweek. March 31,1997).

We can strengthen our hope and perhaps our faith by collecting stories and testimonials to support what we want to believe but to pray: "Oh God, please change the way things are, the way things work, and the way things have always been" seems foolish when we word it this way; but when we pray for specific things or to change the natural order, this is what we are hoping for. If Uncle Fred is within three days of dying from cancer according to the doctors, praying for strength to accept what is likely to happen may be more helpful than praying for something unlikely to happen. Unexpected and unexplained outcomes do happen occasionally, but what we can more easily count on from prayer is a feeling of peace, calm, and being centered emotionally: "Help us to accept the things we do not want but cannot change."

We usually cannot be aware of our connection to the Infinite when we are talking or anxiously working at prayer too hard. We usually cannot feel it when we are thinking. It is when we are quiet that we most powerfully encounter our connection to God. We can feel that we are not emotionally without help or resources to cope, and this is the uniquely human need that prayer fills more than the need for a specific material outcome. Through prayer we encounter our connection to the Universe, and if we choose we can experience it in personal terms. We can interpret it as a feeling that we are loved, that we are cared about, and that we have help to make it through.

Not only is praying for specific outcomes no more helpful than praying for general support, but also the specific form of prayer or who is praying is not critical either. Religious prayers are no more effective than secular ones. It is obvious from our own experience that people who are quite religious in their daily practices of living and praying are no more successful in changing life's events than those who are not. It is pretty clear that even the most religious and devout people get sick and die and prayer doesn't change that. The Universal Agenda is probably more important and powerful than our individual wishes and notions about how things should proceed, whether the request comes from the most or least devout person. It doesn't remove or reverse tragedy nor keep nice people from suffering. It's pretty clear that some of the least religious, and most obnoxious and irritable people sometimes live in good health, with good fortune, to ripe old ages while some of the most devout, good people experience terrible tragedies and early deaths. The Bible reports people in Jesus' time struggling with this same question:

> As he passed by, he saw a man blind from his birth. And his disciples asked him, "Rabbi, who sinned, this man or his parents, that he was born blind? Jesus answered, "It was not that this man sinned, or his parents, but that the works of God might be made manifest in him." (John: 9:1-3)

We don't like accepting that what is, is the expression of God. We want to blame someone for human suffering: the victim for impure thoughts, their family for not having enough faith, the Devil for intervening, God for not being fair. Prayer can't change most of the specific events of our lives, but it certainly can affect how we experience and cope with the events of our lives. We need to be realistic about the possible specific outcomes of our prayers while remaining boundless in the expectation of comfort it can bring.

Perhaps you heard the tale of the camper that illustrates how we already confine our expectations of prayer to a certain set of parameters:

> This camper was out hunting bear with his brand new rifle. He had been out most of the morning, walking up and down the hills and through the brush looking for a bear.

> Unfortunately a huge brown bear spotted him first. With a giant roar the bear started chasing the camper up the hill and down the other side. The hunter discarded his pack. He fell and lost his hat. And finally he even dropped his brand new gun in a desperate attempt to make it to safety. Totally exhausted, the hunter finally fell against the base of a tree. He squinted his eyes together to shut out the sight of the charging bear and called out in prayer:
>
> "Dear Lord, I'm in deep trouble here; if it is your will, please let your divine presence descend on this ugly beast!"
>
> By this time the bear was within one drooling leap of the poor fallen hunter. Just at that moment the divine presence of God did apparently come upon that bear, because just before it leapt on the helpless camper, the bear unexpectedly fell to its knees and said:
>
> "Dear Lord, I thank you for this meal of which I am about to partake."

We smile at the story because even as many of us continue to pray to change things that are pretty likely to happen anyway, we still only expect a certain limited number of outcomes as possible responses to our not so subtle prayer suggestions. The story also twists onto our funny bone because we assume that animals do not speak in human language, have a relationship with God in the same way humans do, nor pray like humans. We are aware, however, of connections non-human animals have to God that we humans have not developed or do not have. The National Park Service annually relocates the infamous bears who get in the garbage cans and hence are a potential threat to human park visitors. Sometimes relocated a hundred miles away, within a few days or weeks, some of these animals are right back playing in the garbage cans and enjoying these heaven-sent gifts. Migratory fish, birds, or swallow tail butterflies who always return to the same area to mate after traveling hundreds or thousands of miles, sometimes through their genetic off-spring, also demonstrate connections with the Source of Creation that humans do not enjoy. All of creation is connected to its source in its own ways. Prayer is a uniquely conscious human experience formed by the possibilities and limitations of our thought processes and emotional needs. What we can reasonably pray for and receive is that our connection with the Source of Creation will continue to nourish and comfort us.

Experiments with Conscious Intention

Some religious believers resist expanding traditional concepts of prayer or resist doing research on its power, because they fear it will undermine both belief and faith; but it seems more likely that research on prayer and the nature of spiritual experience will strengthen not only our understanding but the believability of our spiritual intuitions as well. The Princeton Engineering Anomalies Research Program (PEAR) addressed the kind of research that helps us bring science and prayer together. This program studied telepathic communication and its effects, which is one way of describing what people try to do with intercessory prayer. In intercessory prayer people try to communicate mentally to God to intervene in order to try to get a specific physical or material outcome. The PEAR program studied the success of these attempts without a theological interpretation. Engineers used electronic circuitry to randomly generate pulses that were calculated as either a plus (+) or a minus (-), anywhere from 10 to 10,000 times per second. People in their experiment were successful at making the output of these randomly produced impulse generators contain either more positive or more negative impulses, depending on which one they chose to try to affect through their mental concentration. The effects were small but beyond chance levels of occurrence and were statistically verifiable.

The PEAR program also demonstrated that one individual can communicate or affect the visual images and thoughts of a recipient individual who may be as far away as the other side of the world. We have become accustomed to occasional reports of mental telepathy even if we haven't experienced much of it ourselves. The part we are not accustomed to is that the individuals in these experiments reported by Robert Jahn and Brenda Dunne in Margins of Reality were asked to try to receive messages sent from another individual before it was ever sent—before the sending person had a thought and tried to communicate it, that is, not only outside of space but also outside of time. The 1977 CBS News Magazine filmed one of these experiments and showed a recipient accurately describing a scene of the Rockefeller Chapel at the University of Chicago, one hour and fifteen minutes before the sending person visited that site and then tried to communicate that image telepathically. The site was randomly chosen from a multiple list of city locations in a sealed envelope, the sites being unknown before hand to either the sender or the receiver. This apparently not only documented the occurrence of mental telepathy but also that it can function outside time.

Like most people, I do not have regular telepathic perceptions, but also like many people I have had at least one clear experience in my life that lets me believe that the ability to perceive things at a distance without verbal communication does exist. Many people, especially twins have reported premonitions or vivid dreams of an injury or death of a loved one at the moment the event took place elsewhere in the world. I was in a workshop once with Stanley Krippner whose writings describe many experiences of altered mental states. As a group we decided to try out whether extrasensory perception could occur within our group. We decided that in the evening after our workshop was done for the first day and we had all scattered to various parts of Chicago for the evening, those who were interested or remembered would intentionally try be in a receptive state at 7PM. Stanley said that at 7PM he would consciously attempt to transmit some message from wherever he was and whatever he was doing at the time.

There was no prescribed way to do this nor any clue as to what a "receptive state" was supposed to be, so at 7PM I lay down, went through a quick exercise to relax my muscles and clear my mind, and just waited. Pretty soon I was day dreaming, or sleep dreaming, or something in between. There was a scene, kind of like the mountains of the Alps, in which I was moving toward another figure and then toward a little cottage. There was a pond off to the left where this shepherd stood. It looked as though he belonged to a certain clan because he had a very distinctively radiant shade of deeply rich turquoise in his shirt that was showing through from under his cape. The cottage was a cute brown on white mountain chalet with a thatched roof that was in need of some repair. It vaguely reminded me of some picture of a chalet I'd seen somewhere before. The scene changed a bit to focus on a flock of sheep, and then suddenly it was 7:25. I thought this was an interesting experience, a bit odd that I could just produce a pretty clear scene in my mind at that particular time, but was pleased that at least I had something to describe to the workshop group the next morning.

Well, we all arrived the next morning a bit sleepy. Some had completely forgotten the exercise or to "be receptive", but we were all curious as to what Stanley had been doing the night before at 7PM. Those of us who had anything to report related various stories and descriptions, totally unrelated to each other unless we tried very hard to bend them into some common themes. We then asked what he had actually been concentrating on and trying to communicate to us by mental telepathy. Unexpectedly for me, he had not been out eating or enjoying Chicago, but rather had rested in his room and decided to focus on a specific painting on the wall in the room where he was staying. He brought the painting along so we could all look at it. It was a close up scene of some people on a fishing boat on a very tranquil sea. The content did not seem to have much to do with my images from 7PM the previous night, but I knew instantly that telepathic communication had taken place. The sea in the picture was a very distinctively radiant shade of deeply rich turquoise that I had seen only one other time in my life—in the shirt of the shepherd I had envisioned at 7PM the previous evening!

There have been multitudes of experiments and reports demonstrating this limited human ability to perceive outside our usual cognition and senses. Totally accurate communication does not always occur, or at least it is not always perceived, and it doesn't happen all the time. The transmissions may be incomplete. Portions of an image may be communicated, such as those produced when police use psychics to discover more information about crimes that have been committed. Psychic revelations, however, seem also to be shaped by the diverse influences of our own perceptions, mood, health, memories, and personal issues, as well as what we may have eaten for dinner and what was on the evening news. We have to interpret any such perception through our own consciousness in ways that fit in with our comprehension and understanding. So sometimes intuition and dreams produce information or bits of information that do correspond to conscious perception and reality, past and future, and sometimes perceptions are triggered that have no correspondence at all to any reality we are aware of.

It is this malleable nature of our perception that has led to disallowing testimony in court from witnesses who have been hypnotized and why children who have been "interviewed" by police or social workers looking for a specific answer in criminal investigations have proven to be able to remember very clearly traumatic memories of sexual abuse that never happened. We can remember things that really happened. We can forget things that really happened. We can remember things very clearly that never happened. We can sometimes envision things that haven't yet happened—and sometimes we're completely wrong.

There are some people whom we might call "healers" who feel they not only can perceive information about another person's body at a non-verbal level but also possibly can communicate non-verbally at the same level. These healers feel they can psychically help channel energy from a universal pool into another's body that can assist in healing. Depending on their religious framework these healers often interpret this as God's love, universal energy, or simply intuitively guiding energy to the other person's point of need. Usually such healers express that whatever is going on, they are not the source of the energy, and they are nothing more than channels or a focus of this energy.

When my aching back turned me into a hobbling cartoon character, everyone at our holistic medical center wanted to have a crack at fixing me. I had offers of acupuncture, nutritional supplements, physical exercises to follow, prayer, hypnotic imagery and energy healing. Two different physical therapists evaluated me and made recommendations. Even though my back hurt in the lower right side, they both decided that the problem was in my left abdominal area. One explained it as muscle imbalance where I was compensating too much with my right-sided muscles for weakness on the left. The other didn't explain it at all. She simply held her hands a few inches from my left side and made swirling motions, like she was stirring icing with her finger. I felt a sense of pressure though she never touched me. There was slight discomfort, almost pain under her fingers, which immediately stopped as soon as she stopped her mixing motion. My back got better. Maybe it was one of these activities that helped. Maybe, like most backaches, it would have gotten better in a few days anyway. It certainly feels good to be cared about and (almost) touched and perhaps this accelerated self-initiated healing. While improvement from these kinds of treatments are common, the frequency and success of energy healing remains currently somewhat mysterious and inconsistent. Research on "healing touch" has shown some positive outcomes from people with loving intention moving their hands over the bodies of patients without touching them. (For more information on these studies the reader can consult the work of people such as Dolores Krieger or Janet Quinn.) More investigations of this phenomenon are currently underway. Whatever these activities are, they too seem to be some form of what we can call prayer even though they do not contain verbal language.

Most who have studied or practiced these kinds of healing procedures do not emphasize the form or the technique involved so much as the mental intention to focus caring attention to a suffering person from themselves as well as from the Source of Being. We cannot ignore that some people, when waving their hand around in the air near another person's body, formally praying or just concentrating in a loving way, can apparently sometimes intuit a problem and initiate an effect on the physiological functioning of another person. The research on the effect of prayer on plants, mental telepathy, healing touch, hypnosis and other forms of prayer all point to the fact that our own conscious and unconscious thought can sometimes minimally affect physical change. The problem is that most of us are not able to focus it, control it, nor direct the outcome so it is not much of a factor in our lives if the ability does exist in us at all.

While we need to broaden our concept of what prayer is and how we can apprehend the Infinite, people have not continued to pray over the centuries primarily because of an occasional effect on their material world. People continue to pray because it helps salve our emotional wounds, strengthen our will, and bring comfort to our isolation and despair.

> Prayer is a source as real as a terrestrial gravity. As a physician, I have see men, after all other therapy has failed, lifted out of disease and melancholy by the serene effort of prayer. It is the only power in the world that seems to overcome the so called "laws of nature"; the occasions in which prayer has dramatically done this have been termed "miracles." But a constant, quieter miracle takes place hourly in the hearts of men and women who have discovered that prayer supplies them with a steady flow of sustaining power in their daily lives. Too many people regard prayer as a formalized routine of words, a refuge for weaklings, or a childish petition for material

things. We sadly undervalue prayer when we conceive it in these terms, just as we should underestimate rain by describing it as something that fills the birdbath in our garden. Properly understood, prayer is a mature activity indispensable to the full development of personality—the ultimate integration of man's highest faculties. Only in prayer do we achieve that complete harmonious assembly of body, mind and spirit which gives the frail human reed its unshakable strength.

The words, "Ask and it shall be given to you," have been verified by the experience of humanity. True, prayer may not restore the dead child to life or bring relief from physical pain. But prayer, like radium, is a source of luminous, self-generating energy. How does prayer fortify us with so much dynamic power? To answer this question, I must point out that all prayers have one thing in common. The triumphant hosannas of a great oratorio, or the humble supplication of an Iroquois hunter begging for luck in the chase, demonstrate the same truth: that human beings seek to augment their finite energy by addressing themselves to the Infinite source of all energy. When we pray, we link ourselves with the inexhaustible motive power that spins the universe. We ask that a part of this power be apportioned to our needs. Even in asking our human deficiencies are filled and we arise strengthened and repaired. ("Prayer is Power", Alexis Carrell, M.D., Reader's Digest, 1948.)

The SIH Response

When the doctors fail to heal you,
When the medicine chest can't make you well,
When no counsel leads to comfort…
Let your soul be your pilot.
Let your soul guide you along the way.

("Let Your Soul Be Your Pilot".
Words and music by Sting.)

My body inherited a few small birthmarks and moles when I was born. But then one year, in my late teens, I was the recipient of yet another reminder of my imperfection. No, not the pimples! A wart, about the size of a pencil eraser. Growing right there on the top of my left hand. No one else in my family ever had warts. It was genuinely ugly! My grandmothers were both dead by this time so nobody told me to rub a potato on it and then bury the potato under the eve of the house or other equally proven folk remedies. So the wart and I just lived with each other for a year or so. Not comfortably, however. It's amazing how much we use the back of our hand: for filling up gloves, caressing your girl friend's face, banging on door frames that get too close to your body, offering an acceptable place for your dog to lick you, and a whole host of other under-appreciated activities. There was no need to protect this wart since it didn't hurt except when it got rough and started bleeding from wearing off the skin or if I repeatedly tried to pick it off.

Fortunately, I guess, my girl friend's step-father was a doctor. He said he could take that wart right off. So one weekend we went to his office. He injected the area to numb it and took an electric zapper pen and vaporized it. Over the years the scar has faded quite a bit, though it remains about the size of a shrunken dime. I didn't care for the procedure at all. I hate that burning flesh smell and don't much care for needles and zapping things either. But, no more wart!

A few years later I develop another wart. Guess where? No, not there! On the other hand! To the centimeter, in exactly the same spot where the first one was on the left hand! AMAZING! See the two-headed woman! Gaze in fear at the man who is half alligator! Ease your own sorrow with the man who grew twin warts! How can that be? How can my mind/body-being cause/allow another wart to emerge exactly in the same spot on the other hand? Not a miracle, perhaps, but pretty darn curious. Frankly, for those of us who have not claimed to be abducted by aliens, these kinds of things may be the closest most of us come to a personal experience of the really deep mysteries of the universe. You're unimpressed? There's more…

Easily remembering that burning flesh smell, I lived with this wart even longer. It was even more difficult on my dominant hand to keep from banging, bleeding, and generally irritating it. So finally after three years, enough was enough. I decided to go for the dual scar look. I was now living in Chicago with lots of good dermatologists. At least I guess this one must have been good, because I couldn't get in to see him for six weeks.

Three weeks before the appointment, I thought the wart was not quite as bumpy and scaly. Two weeks before the appointment, it was definitely smaller. It was shrinking! One week before the appointment, I didn't have any wart at all. Health care was more affordable and accessible then and my curiosity was overwhelming, so I went to see the doctor anyway. He wasn't even impressed! He said this happened fairly often and hadn't my grandmother ever told me about rubbing a potato on a wart and burying it under the eve of the house or some other variation of tried and true folk cures that have put a lot of warts to death?

The doctor's more scientific explanation was that warts are caused by low level viral infections. Because they don't endanger the body as a whole, they sometimes can live on the body's surface without the immune system seeming to notice or be alarmed. But when we focus our immune system on the wart by some heightened conscious attention or ritual: Good Guys 1, Wart Hogs 0.

Influencing Healing Through Conscious Intention

I didn't even comprehend at the time what an astounding idea this was: **We can influence our immune system by conscious thought!** Just the statement, let alone the fact that I personally experienced this, is really incredible! It took twenty years for the full appreciation of this experience and what this perceptive dermatologist said to fully impact my thinking. What he was saying was: what we think changes what our immune system does and can help our bodies heal. It is not outside the "natural order", but it is amazing and is enough to reconsider things like prayer and meditation to encourage healing even if you don't "have faith" or believe in a personal God who intervenes in the course of Nature.

Surprisingly, I had one last (I hope) opportunity to experience the Wart Wars. After a few more years, I developed a lump on my left temple. By now, I was ready and eager. I now not only had folk wisdom and medical knowledge, but I also had "modern" psychological weaponry. I had self-hypnosis and healing imagery techniques on my side. Look out, tough guy! I was actually happy to have this innocent little invader to experiment on. So after a few months, to demonstrate that it wasn't going away on its own, I told my wife:

"See this wart thing right here? I'm going to make it go away with self hypnosis."

"Yea, OK. We don't have anything to eat; you want to go out tonight?"

Three weeks! It was gone. I had read the Symingtons' work about trying to assist the body's immune system to kill cancer cells through mental imagery. I had trained in hypnosis and practiced self-hypnosis. I had trained in producing alpha waves with biofeedback. I was as prepared as the United States in the Desert Storm War against Iraq. So after putting myself in a non-thinking relaxed state, and after several kinds of images received a trial run, I settled on this image of an energy gun working from underneath my skin. Targeting a bit of the underneath side of the wart, I fired the gun and vaporized a small part of the unwanted tissue. I could really focus this image clearly in my mind—and, better yet, I didn't have to put up with that burning flesh smell either. I set the image up so that the gun kept firing 24 hours a day even when I wasn't consciously thinking about it. Daily I would focus on the image again and reinforce it's power. The wart began to reduce in size and in three weeks was completely gone.

"Look what I did, Honey! It's gone!"

"That's nice. If you're not so busy now, could you fix the screen door?"

So I proved to myself not only the remarkable, amazing ability of our mind to influence our immune system and direct its healing power when we ask it to, but also learned that you shouldn't use your spouse as the first person to verify your self-proclaimed emergence as a miracle worker. I also learned several other important things about self initiated healing. We don't necessarily have to believe in it or even know about it for it to take place, but our thoughts, emotions, and beliefs seem to be a part of what can influence our self initiated healing. With the first two warts I had no prior belief that I could help produce the removal of the warts by anything I did. That's why I agreed to have them zapped off. Then I had the not so uncommon experience of a self initiated healing (SIH). It was a time when I had no knowledge or expectation of this physical phenomenon changing, so I experienced SIH as more amazing, more surprising, more miraculous. The third time I got a wart, I helped focus SIH deliberately. This phenomenon seems to involve actions beyond what we normally think of as just mental or just physical functions of our body. It can happen with or without conscious intention. It reaches beyond consciousness and taps knowledge and energy to sustain life in ways we don't control. Because of these qualities self initiated healing perhaps can also interchangeably be thought of as spirit initiated healing or soul initiated healing.

Most of the time SIH is completely unconscious. We don't get sick from a lot of things that malfunction in our body, because our body and unconscious intelligence fix most things before we ever have any symptoms. Our immune system kills off foreign invaders and walls off potential threats all the time. I am regularly grateful to my body for doing this for me. My lungs inhaled clouds of asbestos filled air for weeks when I was remodeling old houses filled with asbestos insulated heating pipes that needed tearing out and asbestos filled flooring that needed tearing up. It's been nearly thirty years now and I haven't gotten lung cancer yet. The Good Guys are still ahead. Of course, the asbestos fibers are either in me and walled off or eliminated by now. I didn't know then that asbestos triggers cancer or I would have tried harder not to inhale it; but my body knew, and did what it could to prevent illness. Self or spirit initiated healing takes place all the time, without our consciously knowing it, because we never get any symptoms of illness.

Is the curing of the abnormal cell growth or prevention of cancer significantly different than dealing with warts? Can we consciously use spirit initiated healing to cure cancer or other deadly conditions? The answer is probably a very definitive, absolutely, "sometimes". Cancer and other physical problems aren't just about abnormal cell growth, however. There are other influencing factors. Why did that second wart appear in exactly, to the centimeter, in the same spot as the first one, but on the other hand? This was not an accident. There is some reason, not consciously known to me, why that spot is the appropriate one. These reasons may have to do with unconscious genetic information, my own unconscious memory experience, or emotions that cause a physical reaction in a particular part of my body. The explanation goes beyond the action of the virus and the immune cells which presumably are free to roam about as they see fit. Something else decided where the Wart Wars would take place, something unexpected, unexplainable, and worth exploring.

A number of years ago E. Grey Dimond and his fellow cardiologists at the University of Kansas Medical Center intentionally tried to influence healing by their external medical manipulation. A heart surgery to relieve chest pain had become increasingly popular in which they tied off the internal mammary arteries and veins. This surgery was quite successful in reducing the chest pain of cardiac patients, increasing their ability for physical activity, reducing their need for nitroglycerin, and increasing their over all sense of wellness. But these same results were obtained when all Dr. Dimond did was make a small incision in the skin, expose the same blood vessels, and doing nothing else but sew the patients back up. Typical of the recipients of this sham surgery were one patient's glowing comments:

> "Practically immediately I felt better. I felt I could take a deep breath…I figure I'm about 95 per cent better. I was taking five nitros a day

> before surgery. In the first five weeks following, I have taken a total of twelve." (Dimond, Kittle, and Crocket."Comparison of Internal Mammary Artery Ligation and Sham Operation for Angina Pectoris". American Journal of Cardiology 5, 1960, pp. 483-86.)

Unfortunately, sometimes instead of influencing SIH positively, our surgical attempts to help actually prevent further healing from occurring. If a surgeon removes a piece of herniated disc material that is pushing on a nerve root and causing a feeling of pain in the back and down a leg, there is usually a relief of the pain. When the surgeon takes out that herniated disc, the body doesn't know whether it was stabbed by an attacker, hit by a train, or had what we call "surgery". All it knows is, it has a hole that needs filling up. So it grows scar tissue. It's Nature's own Grandma, just knitting the pieces back together where the surgeon's knife cut and the herniated disc material was removed. If in the process of healing, that scar tissue attaches itself to the nerve root from which we just removed the disc, we are now literally stuck with a permanent pain without a surgical solution for it—though we fixed the original problem. Every time we move, it pulls on the nerve that is now stuck to the scar tissue. It feels again like our leg is on fire, aching, burning, and creating continuing misery. We have then created with surgery and the body's own healing, a problem that can't be fixed. If we do more surgery to remove the scar tissue from the nerve, we have created another hole which the body has to fill by growing even more scar tissue.

Sometimes the best efforts of our body to adjust and heal, leaves us with problems; but it's doing the best it can to help us survive.

Just as doctors and hospitals should not be blamed when we voluntarily seek help that doesn't work as well as we hoped, we should not blame ourselves either. Illness, disease, or failed surgery is not punishment for living wrong. Medical problems occur when the human organism cannot maintain a balance of its own needs within the environment in which we put it or creates a problematic change in our body from the stress of trying to maintain that balance. Sometimes our innate healing capacities can adjust to breathing in cigarette smoke or asbestos; sometimes it cannot, and we become sick or die. Many times we can adjust to the stress of a difficult boss or unloving spouse, sometimes our bodies must sacrifice arteries to maintain the high blood pressure this stress calls forth and we suffer long term chronic illness which eventually could case a fatal occurrence. Sometimes because we don't exercise enough, our innate healing abilities become weakened from disuse. Sometimes we cannot maintain a healthy balance between what's good for our body and the way we live; but this is a result of living. It is not punishment from God for some identified or unidentified sin. Our whole being, mentally and physically through SIH, does the best it can to adjust and cope with the needs of our living.

We know that people who are often angry have to ask their cardiovascular system to work overtime to support and maintain that anger. The result is that they tend to irritate the lining of their blood vessels, cause plaque build up, develop artery disease and narrowing, and are more prone to get heart attacks and die. This doesn't make them bad people. This is just the way their body/mind found to live, even slowly sacrificing their cardio-vascular system if necessary to cope with the hostile world they perceived and lived in it. We also know that the death rate is 30% higher following cardiac surgery for people who do not have a primary loving relationship in their life. That doesn't make these people bad or guilty of not trying hard enough. Their body/minds just have a harder time finding a solution that supports continued healing and life. While we need to be aware of how to assist the healing ability within us, even if we don't eat meat, don't smoke cigarettes, don't live over radon, avoid stress, and exercise every day, we still die. This remembrance that human life consists of the inseparable unity of the mind, body, and a spirit that is supported by the Universal Desire for Existence should not become a new unexamined mythology of denying our mortality. The cemetery business is not going to face a recession in the foreseeable future just because we rediscovered the connection of our mind, body, and spirit.

Placebo = SIH

Because medical science conceptually split the body from the mind, what actually happens in healing has been twisted out of shape to fit our medical model. The placebo response is a good example. We have learned that sometimes things we do help our immune system to focus on a problem and heal it, like rubbing a potato on a wart or giving someone a "sugar pill". Because the body's continued existence depends on its ability to heal itself, it is not surprising that a lot of things can help our body trigger its ability to heal itself.

Modern medical capabilities, however, have sometimes led us to believe that what doctors do is more important than what bodies do for themselves. So when we experience SIH we, along with the medical system, sometimes act as though it is not real healing, or at least a suspect kind of healing. Doctors talk about "placebo responders; it's just a placebo effect; this drug is no better than a placebo; there seems to be a psychosomatic component to this illness; their pain seems to have a functional (psychological) overlay; it's probably just a placebo effect", and a multitude of other comments that under-appreciate or even demean the power of self initiated or spirit initiated healing. Sometimes there is considerable frustration, irritation, and disbelief by medical staff when healing takes place in unexplained ways. Sometimes there is even judgment or criticism that the patient wasn't as ill as the patient claimed or had been misdiagnosed, but these statements come from an under-appreciation of SIH. Likewise, patients correctly resent any implication that it's their fault when our best medical treatments don't work. Medicine has become so technical and scientific that it sometimes emits an unintended arrogance that implies that if it isn't a recognized and accepted medical treatment that helps someone become healthier, then it is something to be denigrated or even attacked instead of celebrated. Our advancements in medical science are tremendously beneficial to our society and individuals, but both patients and doctors tend to give too much credit to doctors when patients get better and too much blame when they don't.

A drug company not so long ago developed a new drug to reduce herpes zoster outbreaks. When one of their studies showed that the comparison placebo pill worked better than their new drug, they decided to run a new study on the placebo in hopes of getting a patent for using it for treating herpes zoster. In the new trials, however, the placebo was then referred to as a "promising new treatment possibility". Placeboes, or "sugar pills" with some non-active ingredients, have consistently produced improvement in a wide variety of illnesses 30-35% of the time. New drugs are always tested to see if they can do better than SIH. Sometimes we seem to forget the importance of SIH by our infatuation with outside influences on healing. All healing is internal and outside influences either aid or get in the way of that process. The desire for maintaining health and well being comes built into us, along with the gift of life, part of the desire of the Universe. It is estimated that 50 to 70% of all visits to primary care physicians are for illnesses that have some emotional or stress related cause. Some of them can become life threatening. In the majority of cases our physical symptoms are just symptoms of living, symptoms that our body shows as it uses all its resources to find a way to cope with and sustain our lifestyle as long as it can. Many times all we have to do is stop and rest and our bodies and minds heal themselves.

Instead of an appropriate humbleness in the face of the power and wisdom of our bodies, unhealed patients are often sent to people like me for psychological evaluation to get a diagnostic label that says the reason this stubborn body is not healing in spite of our best medical treatment is because the patient is consciously or unconsciously causing it, faking it, is seriously stressed, or mentally ill. Some of the time psychological stress does lead to physical problems, and whether it is an obvious cause or not, we can often help people maximize their ability to heal themselves through psychological counseling or spiritual direction. It is unenlightened to ask, as some doctors still do, whether this patient's illness or pain is "real". Of course it is, because all illness always has mental, physical, and spiritual components.

The word "psychosomatic" has too often been used to imply that the disease or symptoms the person is having is somehow not real, made up, in the person's head, or not worthy of treatment by "real medicine"; but all illness is always both physical and mental.

> **psychosomatic**: 1. Pertaining to the mind and body. 2. Indicating illnesses in which some portion of the etiology is related to emotional factors.
>
> When so used the impression is created that the mind and body are separate entities and that a disease may be purely somatic in its effect or entirely emotional. This partitioning of the human being is not possible; thus no disease is limited to only the mind or the body. A complex interaction is always present even though in specific instances a disease might on superficial examination appear to involve only the body or the mind.

(Taber's Cyclopedic Medical Dictionary, Edition 13.)

All healing is a miraculous joy to be appreciated by those who experience it. The will and knowledge of how to stay alive comes with the gift of life itself. Human life somehow survived on Earth for several million years without modern medical science, and SIH continues to be the primary cause of bodies repairing themselves. Let us rejoice in this wonder and give thanks!

Most people have never stopped thinking of themselves or experiencing themselves as whole beings of mind, body, and perhaps spirit too. They are sometimes more wise and polite than our medical system. Not wanting to offend their physicians by saying they have failed to help them, nor that they believe in healing methods other than what their doctor uses, nor be denied by their insurance company for filing a claim for an "uncovered" method of healing, many people simply go to alternative practitioners, don't tell their doctors, and don't file insurance claims. In fact in the 1990s there were more visits in the United States to alternative medicine practitioners each year than there were to all the traditional internal medicine and family practice doctors combined. (David Eisenberg, et. al. 1993. "Unconventional Medicine in the United States." New England Journal of Medicine 328: 246-252.)

This is not to suggest that traditional medical treatments should be ignored, even though ironically what we call "traditional medicine" in this country is less than 100 years old and keeps changing all the time, while what we have called "non-traditional medicine" sometimes represent techniques thousands of years old. Sometimes there is an unwarranted backlash or fear against more modern medical methods or taking pills, almost a feeling on the part of some of moral superiority or better healing if we don't take prescription medication. Some people want only "natural ingredients" or "organic foods", implying that those chemicals are somehow better than chemicals the medical system offers. So they will eat anything that was grown in horse manure but would not go near something produced in a sterile laboratory! We should consider carefully whether what we do is likely to promote SIH or interferes with our body's own natural healing, but let's not start with preconceived prejudice. We should try new technologies to promote healing, but recognize that just because it is new or technological in design, does not mean it will always aid our body in healing nor that old "natural" ways are always better.

Besides being realistic about our medical interventions, it also seems prudent to consider adding non-traditional treatments such as hypnosis, mental imagery, massage, prayer, meditation, herbs, vitamins, energy work, nutritional supplements and other approaches to protect healthy cells from invasive medical procedures and toxic agents. If we are going to use methods of healing that also attack the body's ability to maintain its own integrity and SIH, then we are probably best served by using the available complementary techniques to support SIH and control the damage. If our ability to heal ourselves is destroyed, so are we, no matter what methods we used.

Techniques to Encourage SIH

Sometimes we can help maximize self initiated healing through the use of various techniques. Tribal or clan ceremonies led by "witch doctors" (another demeaning name reflecting our irritation with healing we didn't understand), shamans or priests sometimes help maximize healing energies. It is sometimes helpful for someone not just to believe that their body has the ability to heal itself, but to go through a ceremony to help focus SIH through the power of communal support, intention, energy, and expectation. Medical rituals such as getting a prescription and filling it or having surgery are also sometimes helpful. Healing prayer services, exorcisms, and doctor visits themselves can all help encourage SIH.

Another interesting method for promoting SIH is conscious mental focus through the use of hypnosis, mental imagery, and prayer. We have some limited ability to consciously communicate with our body's unconscious knowledge and healing abilities, learn from it, work with it, and encourage more wholeness of mind, body, and spirit. Todd is an example. He had severe pneumonia as a child, and because of the lung scarring and a subsequent occurrence of pneumonia in later life as an adult, he was dependent on 4 liters of oxygen a day to assist his breathing. A medical researcher, he knew how things worked at the cellular level; but when we did some mental imagery, a form of hypnosis or altered state of consciousness, he discovered his mind imagined that he had a forklift in the middle of his left lung. As a scientist this was a stupid idea, but because he produced the imagery himself he was open to the possiblity that his body was trying to tell him something about what was going on in his lungs. The knowledge his body had could be symbolized to his conscious mind as a forklift in a dark, cavernous area. He kept having to hold off the conscious pictures of human tissue he had studied in textbooks and seen under microscopes to let the unconscious knowledge of his body communicate it to his conscious mind in their common language of imagery.

His mind produced the image of large double doors completely blocking the entrance to his right lung. These doors were solidly locked and when he put his face by the keyhole he felt air blowing out the crack between the doors and at the bottom. No air could go in. This was the mental image corresponding to his physical problem of not being able to get enough oxygen to this lung. He mentally pulled and pushed on those imaginary doors. He looked for a key and tried to see through the crack. His logical, conscious solution to his breathing problem was to get those doors open. He even got angry at himself for not working hard enough with his imagery to get those doors open. It took some time for Todd to consider that the unconscious wisdom of his body might have those doors locked for a reason. He stopped fighting with the doors and instead sat quietly in front of them, waiting for understanding.

What he learned was that he didn't have to go through the doors to get to the other side into his lung. He just transported himself behind the doors with his imagination without opening them. Behind the doors, inside his lung, he discovered a laboratory very similar to the one in which he used to work 30 years earlier. Because of their experiments there, they needed positive pressure always blowing out of the lab to prevent any contamination from entering. They also had hoods covering their experiments which were vented out of the room because they worked with chemicals that might be harmful if inhaled. The doors to the lab were always closed because of safety and purity precautions. This seemed to explain why the doors blocking his lung in his imagery were closed and air was always blowing out through them. Rather than continuing to complain about the doors not opening, Todd became a curious, though somewhat still amazed learner from his unconscious mind/body images.

He explored the imagined laboratory inside his lung. Though he could not get the hood over the experiment to open, he recognized the nature of the experiment going on under the protective vented hood. About a month later when we were talking about the meaning of this imagery, he remembered a phone call that he had gotten from the director of the lab some years after he had stopped working there. The director was calling all the former employees with the shocking news that subsequent experiments showed that they had all been exposed to an extremely potent carcinogenic without their knowing it at the time. This dangerous chemical was the very experiment that was being worked on under the vented hood in the imagined laboratory in his right lung. His conscious and unconscious knowledge were beginning to come together!

While his conscious mind was aggravated with his body for closing off this lung and making it more difficult for him to take in air, his unconscious mind had apparently found a way to save his life by closing off the air intake to his previously pneumonia weakened lung when it was exposed to a dangerous carcinogen. The cost of remaining alive was to sacrifice part of the function of his body. This common SIH solution, discovered through his own mental imagery, may not accurately describe all the detail or explanation for what actually went on physically in his lungs, but it offered an amazing intuitive insight into decisions about adapting and staying alive that had apparently been made at the unconscious cellular level of his body, with wisdom and knowledge far beyond his conscious thoughts.

Todd's imagery slowly changed over time. He repeatedly returned to his unconscious knowledge and images. He became more of a partner in working with his body rather than berating it for letting him down and telling it how his imagery should look. His right lung began to get larger and expand more in his imagery, now that his unconscious mind understood that the danger was past. His left lung began to appear lighter in color in his mental images, the forklift became very tiny, and he breathed more easily. In fact, he felt better than he had in years. His physician could not explain why his pulmonary studies showed he was able to take in and use more oxygen with each breath and still initially felt that he should stay on his oxygen tank 18-24 hours a day for the rest of his life. But Todd felt much better, some days wasn't using any supplemental oxygen at all, and was now using oxygen primarily during his new ability to work out on the treadmill for 20 minutes every day.

The real power of healing imagery comes not from our conscious desires but from the fact that our conscious thoughts can interact to a limited degree with our powerful, unconscious self-sustaining mechanisms for life. We may know, for instance, from studying or looking at pictures what the heart or brain or muscle looks like. So when we try to imagine the controlling mechanisms of our mind or physical body, we may try to visualize a picture of a real brain or a heart. We may have difficulty suspending the rigidity of our concrete knowledge, or what we know as facts, or what emotionally we think is right for our bodies or our lives. But unless we are open to more than what we already know, we cannot let a different kind of knowledge emerge from our own spiritual nature and the Spirit of Creation itself. If we are to consciously receive information at all from the knowledge and spirit within our bodies, we have to create a neutral canvass of consciousness and emotion. The knowledge and awareness of our most basic cellular mind can sometimes brush up against that canvass from the other side. When we look at that painting from the framework of our consciousness, we take those images and smears and try to understand them by shaping them into things that we can consciously recognize and appreciate, just as we do every time we have any encounter with the workings of God.

The Universal SIH

Not just our bodies but all Being has this built in character to sustain and regenerate itself, even when it has to alter its function to maintain existence. What is interesting to notice about the loss of the effectiveness of penicillin as various strains of bacteria have become immune to it, is that self initiated healing takes place in other life forms as well as in human beings. We thought that tuberculosis bacteria would die out and go away completely because we discovered penicillin kills it. Of course it will try to find a way to survive. It has the ability not only to alter and heal itself, but to do so in the face of extremely powerful threats to its existence. So now there are new strains of TB that no longer are destroyed by penicillin. Should we be surprised that All of Existence is as equally resourceful as the human body?

SIH is essential to the continuation of being, to change, adapt, evolve, and survive. Not just living beings, but Being itself, has to be able to evolve, regenerate, and mutate in order to remain in existence. Spirit seems as good a name as any to call this universal force to maintain existence. Many different religious traditions recognize, name, and honor this force. It is more than the mechanistic interactions of germs and immune cells that we think of as attacking and defending in our bodies. It is more than mind or consciousness. Spirit is the knowledge and energy in and around matter, allowing adaptation, evolution and change that makes the continuation of existence possible. Each time this Spirit learns and adjusts to a new set of circumstances it evolves into a slightly different, perhaps more advanced form. The Spirit eternally evolves in its ability to support and maintain existence.

Necessarily, Being finds a way to perpetuate itself. Within us, we have enormous resources for healing ourselves and sustaining life, until we must relinquish our time of being, so that Being can continue to be expressed, in a slightly altered form or off-spring, the Universe and God having continued by the experience of our one life. SIH in us represents the ability to renew our own existence but also represents the action of the Universal Spirit to maintain its Existence. Together they are uniquely a single beautiful expression of the Infinite, one and One.

Why Bad Things Happen

Our deepest fear is not that we are inadequate.
Our deepest fear is that we are powerful beyond measure.
It is our light not our darkness that most frightens us.
(Nelson Mandela: Inauguration Speech)

The Theological Problem With Evil

An airplane crashes into a mountainside in South America. Almost all of the 100 passengers are killed, except one family of four who survived. The coincidences of nature came together in a totally unexpected way so that four people, in the same family, survived the plane crash when everyone else was killed. This cannot be God's punishment of those who died nor a special reward for those who lived. "God's will" is an unsatisfactory and uncomfortable way of explaining why events like this happen. We cannot say it's God's will that these people on the plane died and turn around and proclaim that God is a good, loving, and caring life-sustaining presence for us. Our choices in connecting statements about God to bad things that happen seem to be:

1. God is loving but not all powerful. God is incapable of preventing bad things or another equally strong force causes them.
2. God is loving but allows bad things to happen to people who break the rules—and everyone does, so everyone experiences bad things.

3. God created everything but has no active direction or intervention in why things happen now.
4. God is a metaphorical creation for our intellectual, emotional and spiritual awareness of being connected to all the knowledge, matter, and energy of creation but it has nothing to do with why things happen in our lives—but can comfort our pain.

These are all a kind of expression of faith that help us deal with suffering and pain, but do not adequately and honestly explain why a particular event took place. So what did make the plane crash? The analytical answer is "turbulence". All the investigators and the FAA would agree. What caused the family to survive? The analytical answer is that they were sitting where, because of the laws of physics, they were protected from some of the major impact of this particular crash. A metaphorical explanation would be that the Devil reached out his hand and cursed that airplane and the one family survived because God protected them.

But all of those thoughts leave us with an awkward uncertainty about how to respond to these people whose loved ones died. To the families of those who died on the plane, some might offer the simple but discomforting: "It was God's will." A few unsympathetic strangers might suggest it was God's punishment for their sins. But these are insensitive, cruel, and unnecessary responses. They happen because we try to use our religious or metaphorical language to explain why physical events happen rather than confine it more appropriately to expressions of emotional needs and support.

Obviously it is inappropriate and pretty pathetic solace to the parent of a five year old who is struck and killed by a car to say "It is God's will". Parents are not comforted when told this as an explanation for why their daughter was gang raped or their son was killed by a drunken driver. It is not just a logical conclusion that metaphorical and religious language should not be used for scientific or analytical purposes. It's important for our being sensitive to the emotional needs and pain of those who suffer that we not mix up these languages nor use them inappropriately. We should use metaphorical and religious language to comfort, to bring support and caring to those who suffer, with metaphors such as "God is still here for us" or even the sometimes questionable, "God doesn't give us more than we can handle". Sometimes it might be more helpful to just say "I'm sorry life has dealt you this terrible sorrow. I am here for whatever I can do to help." We need to leave our theological metaphors out of analytical and scientific explanations and use them to comfort each other in our trials and suffering.

By the time I was a child, the myth of a powerful, evil Devil was already a joke. The figure with horns, a pitchfork, and a pointy tale became a cartoon or Halloween character because it was obviously a failed metaphorical attempt to explain why bad things happen. "The Devil made me do it" was used more for humor or an easy excuse than an expression of fear or serious explanation. Except for a small minority of intellectually uncomplicated theologies, this left over character from multi-god pantheons is not used much any more to explain why bad things happen. But the Devil's demise, and his rather unsuccessful and abortive theological career, leaves an unexplained gap in popular American religious and theological constructs: If there is no Devil, no universal evil force to cause it, why do bad things happen and people do terrible things? Just as perplexing, why do good things happen to people no better than us?

Some professional football players, who are paid millions of dollars to catch a little ball and score a touchdown in one of the innumerable Sunday games, sometimes suddenly kneel down in the end zone or point to the sky. This appears to be some sort of religious tribute. The now outlawed dancing in the end zone and taunting the opponents seem to be a more appropriate gesture for the celebration of victory in this "game". If we try to apply this end-zone theology in equal analytical terms, we would have to conclude that God punished those bad men on the other team and that he unfairly allowed a special blessing to come into one player's life. If you or I caught the ball, it would be closer to a special blessing or the breaking of the laws of nature, but when a professional football player catches a ball, it was because he's practiced doing this very thing for thousands of hours and gets paid an unbelievable amount of money for doing this "job". Practice in catching little balls and other known laws of the universe are adequate explanations for how touchdowns are scored. References to a divine force aren't really necessary or relevant.

Some people still halfheartedly, or more fervently, mouth the solution that our enemies and other bad people will get their "just rewards" in an afterlife. The idea that our enemies and other nearly as repugnant sinners are just as loved and accepted by the Almighty is a pretty powerful, but sometimes difficult concept to accept. It goes against our sense of fairness. We would rather say that God loves us all, the saint and the sinner—but the brothers and sisters we don't like are surely going to burn in Hell, even if we have to wait a very long time to see justice prevail. But there is no evidence to say that your good life gains any more attention or condemnation from the Source of All Creation than my sinful little existence down the street. Nor is there any evidence of an afterlife where we can be sure we will all get what we think is deserved.

Different world religions have struggled with this issue and have used a variety of ways to explain evil and the occurrence of bad things in life. Oriental philosophy refers to an imbalance of Chi or the Confucian concept of a person being out of balance with their social role. Buddhism solves the problem of evil by saying it's not really necessary to experience these disappointments if we stop striving so hard, that we will eventually escape the imperfections of creation and can escape into calm enlightenment or Nirvana. The biblical Old Testament solution was to blame human behavior. God created a perfect world, but Eve broke the rules, ate the forbidden fruit, and got Adam to do the same thing. So God punished humans forever by making men work in the fields and women have pain in childbirth, pay-back for bad behavior. In Judeo-Christian history the remnants of a warrior-like god who was vengeful with even his own people if they didn't obey the rules was softened by Christian teachings of God as a forgiving and all-loving figure.

Much of American Christianity has decided to believe that the concept of a totally powerful, totally loving god is so important and emotionally satisfying that it can ignore the lack of a good explanation for why bad things happen. Christianity's powerful appeal is the message of the equal value of each individual person, no matter what we've done or what our life has been like. No matter what, you are accepted. God loves you! The central development in Christian doctrine is that the love of God is encompassing, that we don't have to do a single thing to get it or earn it—just accept it. In secular language this means that we all come from the Oneness which gives all life and being, and we're always equally a part of the One, saints or sinners. This fits well with what we experience. Unless their own behavior kills them, people who do bad things also perpetuate themselves, accumulate wealth, enjoy pleasures, and can live as long as the people who do good deeds. The gift of life and being is given equally to everyone. The difference comes in what we decide to do with the gift, for that creates the meaning of our lives.

We cannot escape the "why am I here" question. Unless we inject a set of values and goals into our life, it has no purpose, no road signs, no direction, no meaning. It is too aimless and sometimes too overwhelming to try to cope with the bad things that happen without an overall sense of purpose, direction, or rules to live by to help stabilize ourselves during life's myriad of challenges. Life is really hard on us sometimes. Much of the quality of our life is determined by surrounding circumstances, genetics, chance, and luck. Many of us grew up being loved and taught to act responsibly and caring, sometimes even getting the recognition of our community for doing so. No matter how good our life is, however, we still struggle with the realization that the bad things that happen to us sometimes have no logical reason nor purpose. No Ultimate Personality seems to direct our fate, intervene for our success or failure, nor watch what happens to us. We interpret events that happen as though the universe cared or was angry with us because we need to maintain hope and try to make emotional sense out of things that happen to us. We reach out emotionally and intellectually for personal reassurance from the Ground of Our Being that will ease the loneliness and struggle of being alive.

Whether a person is a theist or an atheist we either have to make a decision to live by some guidelines or simply use up some air until we die. We can just allow our survival genetics to play themselves out—a life without conscious purpose. In the face of there being no clear evidence that there is a great plan, no evidence that anyone other than ourselves is planning our life course or that of the universe, no evidence that bad things that happen to us have any ultimate cause or purpose, we stand alone to make our own faith proclamation as to the value and meaning of our life. We have the opportunity to try to reduce the bad in this world by our commitment to how we will live and by the values we embrace and promote. The presence of evil and injustice that sometimes swirl around us can dominate our daily lives and our emotional and spiritual mood like a daily dose of local TV "news". It requires a conscious commitment to bring about more good than bad in our lives and on our planet. We have been given the opportunity to transcend random disasters and uncaring behavior by embracing values and principles that provide meaning, direction and order to this otherwise chaotic, short-term event in the universe we call our lifetime.

Evil is the Price of Existence

Human life, like all other existence, is an individual manifestation of the paradox of Creation. Without the violent, divisive force, the Perfect Oneness could not have exploded into existence. That same aggressive force necessary for existence is necessary for survival, including human life. So it is Creation itself that is the source of both our appreciation of our oneness and the same source of our ability to destroy each other, our search for love and closeness as well as our desire for independence, our sense of our unity and of our own self-centeredness.

Humans, like many other animals, only survived as a species because we had a certain level of violence and aggression. Our species learned to kill and dominate other animals to gain and protect our food, our territory, and our lives. Aggression has been a necessary part of the continuation of human life. So sometimes we do bad things to other people or parts of creation. Our impulse to work cooperatively and to love and nurture our children so that there will be succeeding generations also had to be supported by a certain amount of toughness and willingness to destroy. We knew or learned to fight off other animals who wanted to eat our food or us, bashing many of them into oblivion or running them off when they got in the way of our farms, towns, villages, and cities. This was not initially a moral issue, just the process of the human race trying to survive and eventually dominating on Earth. If we did not have these traits, there would be no human beings on Earth. The fact that there is aggressive, self-serving behavior as well as communal instinct is not in itself a matter for moral judgment since we could not have been here without both of them. Moral judgments, however, come when we have alternative methods of reaching our survival goals without harming or destroying our environment, other species, or our fellow humans. Moral judgments come when we are capable of meeting our own needs and providing for those of others without destroying our environment or taking advantage of other animals and people.

Too little energy and aggression and humans do not survive. But too much, and we also do not flourish. Someone else with equally strong aggression sees to that. We bemoan conditions in some countries and in some American homes and streets where the skills needed for survival from the dangers exceed the nurturing possibilities. Ultimately this situation cannot support human growth. We have seen some of our communities deteriorate as some vandalize their neighbors, and those who can, leave to a more gentle location. We will probably never evolve to the point where destructive human aggression can be totally eliminated, but we are slowly moving away from the necessity of so much aggression simply for survival and toward the fact that the world community won't tolerate aggressive behavior if it threatens to expand beyond limited localities. Survival of the human species, and perhaps life on the planet will continue to rest on controlling rather than a complete elimination of aggression. Many monastics praying on a hillside retreat or couch potatoes soaking up cathode rays will not save us from the asteroids that will sometime threaten life on our planet. We will need human warriors to take on that battle. On the other hand they need to be contained and balanced so they don't blow up our trade and governmental centers or commit genocide on whole cultures and nations of people. We will always struggle with balancing the assertiveness necessary for our individuality with the sacrifice needed for our inter-dependence.

Our price for being is to become physically and emotionally separated. To be born is to become separate. It is our modern equivalent of the Adam and Eve story. The Biblical account of mankind's separation from God is attributed to Adam and Eve breaking God's rules and eating from the forbidden fruit tree. Without the mythological explanation, "original sin" is really the individuation and separation necessary for being. Humankind is not separate from the Oneness of God because of choice, nor because we have sinned or broken some rule, but because separation is necessary for existence. This is true whether we mean the individuation of cells dividing, separation from the womb, or becoming our own selves as an adult. Our emotional and spiritual development determines whether we widen or close the distance between ourselves and the source of our creation. For us to become who and what we are fully capable of will never allow escape from the struggle of unity and creation, good and evil, togetherness and aggression, connection and separation, but we do have important choices we can make.

When I was young and even more insecure, I did what was expected: went to church, Boy Scouts, and got on the Dean's list. Dated a girl who was the same—well, she was in synchronized swimming instead of Boy Scouts. Dated this same girl through high school and college and did what was expected. Got married. Next step, babies. Wait a minute! Something is wrong here! There I was, someone who had been too afraid to even try dating someone else, who had never had the courage to do one thing that went against what I was told was the right thing to do, acting as though I had the maturity to raise babies! I hadn't even grown up yet, had no idea what I was really like myself, and yet somehow had "given myself" to another person in marriage and was at risk of reproducing!

Here was the first real ethical, moral decision to make in my life—instead of just doing what was expected in order to be doing the right thing. Was I going to end a marriage without apparent problems in order to go out and give myself time to grow up, or was I never going to grow up, stay married, have children, and just keep doing the right thing? It's too easy to say both could happen. I didn't think so then, nor now, and had to choose. People don't reach moral maturity until they are willing to risk being wrong about really important choices. I chose to end a good marriage to a person I admired (I hadn't learned how to love yet) and go find out what I would be like if I made my own choices, and possibly made some mistakes. In order to do so I had to hurt a lot of people I cared about:

My mother: Who was devastated by her son's producing the first divorce in the history of her family and, to her mind, had apparently raised an insane son.

My wife: Who was a very good person whom I cared about and to whom there was no adequate explanation nor apology.

My father: My role model. Thank God he was dead already—though perhaps he was the only one who could have helped me forgive myself sooner.

Grandma: Who loved me like I was her own and whom I was too embarrassed to face.

My in-laws: Who were closer than my own family and who were lost forever.

My family: Who up until then could admire me and be proud of my successes.

Church members: Who hoped at least the ministers would uphold traditional values.

Myself: Who had to break the first two identified values about who I hoped I would become:

1. Always keep my word—so much for "I do, I will, and I won't ever…"
2. Treat people with love and respect—so much for not hurting people you care about.

It was the first hard moral choice I ever made, the first step to real maturity, at a terrible cost. I hurt a lot of people and caused a lot of suffering to those I cared about. I caused myself immense anguish and pain. I could have made the other choice and stayed married. But I believed I acted with the highest form of morality, because I considered the choices carefully, including the hardship on others, made the decision thoughtfully, and accepted the consequences. If my life was going to crash straight into a ditch, at least I could say that I was finally steering it myself.

As in most difficult moral choices, there was not a clear good vs. evil choice here. Being a good person is more than doing the right thing. It was bad to throw away the life-gift to become whatever I could fully become as a person, but also bad to hurt people who didn't deserve it. Bad things sometimes come out of the process of individuation. Bad things sometimes flow from the nature of creation and of continuing existence. Just as the All had to split apart in order to come into existence, we have to separate from the physical and emotional dependency of our childhood in order to fulfill our own possibility and potential. The price of fulfilling the potential of our own creation is the tension, conflict, and sometimes pain of becoming more separate. When anything comes into being, the creating force no longer controls it, even though the separate new bit of creation could not exist without the basic matter and energy supplied by the creator. It is the act of coming into existence itself, that introduces imperfection, imbalance, conflict, and bad things, especially when the created being, such as humans, have so much ability to influence and shape their own existence.

We are tempted to hope that evil could be avoided in a perfect world, but in our world it is just part of the consequence of existence.

The force that creates the separation required for being, always contains an underlying tension between reunifying and separating further. The source of destructive behavior and natural disasters are the same forces necessary for creation and survival. In order for there to be anything other than the original Oneness of all matter, energy, and knowledge, it had to come apart. For individual things and pieces to exist and remain, they have to be driven by energy, sometimes eating, destroying, or using up other beings or resources in order to stay separate and exist. Human beings are part of that same process of coming into being, struggling to fulfill our potential, then losing our organizing life force and dying, existence sustained only through influencing the next generation, value and importance imparted only by the choices we make. Birth is our own personal experience of separation. Death is being reabsorbed. A full and ethical life is one which balances between being too separate and too dependent.

How We Overcome Evil

If there are no great cosmic good and evil personalities, no great plan for our existence, no one in charge of life except us, dealing with evil is first a matter of dealing with ourselves. We have to make some deliberate commitment to what we are going to with our own agression, if we are going to let more goodness than evil come from us and affect our world. The most powerful ethical issue for human beings is that we are given the ability, right, and responsibility to make our own decisions about how we act. We can love people and can hurt people, and will sometimes have difficult choices about it. Sometimes we will have to act aggressively to eliminate other specific aggressive individuals from our society who do damage and spread harm to others, even while we know that we are not perfect ourselves.

Good and bad, and choices about, it will be part of our life experience. We can get depressed about it, afraid, angry, or try to ignore it. Or, we can embrace this one-lifetime opportunity and live it to our very best. It won't be perfect; but it doesn't have to be. As long as it is our best, we can embrace it with honor. Whatever principles and values we choose is our statement about the nature of God. Whatever lifetime we splatter on the universal canvass is a prized expression of Creation and it is our contribution to the masterpiece of eternity. It is the statement made by how we live that overcomes the emotional isolation of our creation, the fear that our life has no purpose, and transcends the suffering from the bad things that inevitably come into our lives. It is also our statement as Co-Creators in the Universe that the primary nature of God in us is the desire for good.

There is no evidence that we'll be punished or rewarded in an after-life for the choices we make, but how we live our lives does affect Eternity. Some of us will live lucky lives, lots of food, lots of love, fewer difficulties, generally free of illness and pain. Some of us are unlucky, lots of abuse, disappointments, struggles, and a body that should have been covered by a lemon law. But we are all equal parts of Creation. The factor that provides stability in our ups and downs is our mental outlook, our core values, our thoughtful choices, our committed decisions, our faith. A person of faith decides to live to the highest values he or she can conceive. A person of faith deliberately decides how they want to use these precious moments of awareness we have been given as a gift. Our choices, decisions, and commitments are our personal statement about the meaning and purpose of life. It is our decisions and commitments that lift us above our ability just to fight for survival, that tempers our necessary aggression, and allows goodness to dominate. Perhaps, if enough people do this thoughtfully, we will shape life on our planet, and even infinitesimally nudge the Universe toward a slightly higher plane; but if not that grand goal, we have created a meaning, even honor, for this one life, in this one place. The ultimate challenge of life is what we decide to do with the time between our birth and our death. It is our own glorious moment to proclaim the purpose of our life and the possibility of God:

> **I believe the world is a better place if we live our lives with kindness and respect. In the face of unpredictable disasters, personal pain, the cruelty of others, and my own foolishness, I will nourish my faith and commit myself to live with love and caring. Though I sometimes fail to live up to my own ideals, I will always live the best I can. To live my best is why I am here, always deserving of respect from both myself and others. I will live a life that brings honor both to my own existence and to all Creation. I believe when we share this commitment together, we transcend our separateness, overcome our fears, and join in Spirit. Amen.**

Before and After Life

> The world is so exquisite with so much love and moral depth, that there is no reason to deceive ourselves with pretty stories for which there's little good evidence. Far better it seems to me, in our vulnerability, is to look death in the eye and to be grateful every day for the brief but magnificent opportunity that life provides. (Carl Sagan. Skeptical Inquirer. Vol 21, No. 2. March/ April 1997. "Tribute to Carl Sagan".)

The Only Problem With Death Is....

The biggest problem we have with accepting that our existence ends with death is that we want to avoid dealing with the uncomfortable possibility that our individual lives might not be important. So we're looking for something that will transform this gloomy fear. For most of us our lives are individually important only to us and a few other people. Wrapping this harsh reality in the hope for an afterlife does not make it any different. The concept of an afterlife, while meant to be comforting, ironically turns our living into a warm up lap for the real thing. It actually detracts from the important business of this life. If we don't like the way we live or the circumstances of our current life, the concept of an afterlife is a comforting concept. But in providing this tranquilizer, we diminish the importance of our current choices. We help proclaim the meaning of our own life either by de-emphasizing the importance of this life or holding it with final reverence. We glorify the importance of our life and honor its sacredness more by emphasizing this as our single chance to manifest the nature of God in us, than we do by suggesting that if we misplay this one, we'll get a mulligan.

The Universe does not need any one of us in order to survive or expand—there are plenty more eggs and sperm and cells to clone from where we came. But the Universe <u>is</u> forever shaped and changed by the fact that we have lived and the choices we make. Our individual lives are not a necessary part of creation or evolution, but once we came into being, we do shape the nature of the Universe. We are a manifestation of the Creation of God. Isn't that special enough? Do we need the comfort of another life, if we embrace this one as our gift to and from God?

Speculative conjectures about Heaven and Hell are sometimes cited as reasons for doing or not doing things in this life. These concepts are practically irrelevant to most people's daily lives and decision making. The thought that this is the only life we're going to get and we won't get another chance, that today is the only today we're ever going to get, ought to be more powerful ethical and spiritual motivation than speculation about a reward in some other life. If we don't think we're going to get another chance, we better be very careful that we do it right this time. Letting go of the idea of an afterlife is both frightening and liberating. Sometimes life is pretty tough. Broken hearts, bones, and promises abound, and it's difficult to cope. Other times are pretty joyous. Neither times are particularly deserved. We do, however, have the power to direct the part of our lives we can control: how we will treat others, interact with our environment, set our goals, and spend our energies. What a wonderful, glorious, fantastic surprising opportunity to have this one day, this one life, and to decide how we will use it. Is there really a need to imagine another lifetime if we're satisfied with how we've lived this one?

Spirits and Souls

Our personality and our individual manifestation of Spirit (Chi, Prana, Vital Force) only exists because our unique collection of cells and matter came together. There is little to suggest that our personalities continue after we die without a material body to support us. Many people want the reassurance of an afterlife and just choose to believe in it, no matter if the idea doesn't meet standards of evidence they demand everywhere else in their lives. There are a few people who claim an experience of seeing or talking with dead relatives, having had a near death experience, mediums who seem to connect mentally to spirits of dead people, and people who claim to have been abducted by creatures from another planet. All of these experiences seem to be shaped by the personality and emotional needs of the people experiencing them and does not lead to the conclusion that we all have a non-material personality that eludes physical death.

Some people claim to have memories of past lives. These are probably products of our own human projection and fertile imagination. Americans who claim to remember a past life almost always seem to recall one where they spoke English and had a culture with which we are familiar from history books. That seems overly coincidental. If reincarnation takes place, can we only be reborn in a country that speaks our same language? And if spirits are reborn, why would previous lives, or future lives for that matter, be as a human being? Why not reincarnation as a frog, or a Canadian goose, or a magnolia tree, or a spirit in another dimension than ours? And why would we be reborn on the planet Earth, in this solar system? Getting another lifetime is one of those fantasies that (perhaps fortunately) may be too good to be true. Of all the things that influence our daily decision making and moral choices, the fear of being reborn as a turkey vulture if we don't live correctly is probably one we're better off not having to consider.

Beef stew, on the other hand, perhaps can help teach us something about encounters with non-material personalities. Before it was stew there were carrots, and onions, and chunks of beef, and tomatoes and other things that the cook threw in. When they were all chopped up and cooked together they all take on a new taste and texture. Sometimes when we fish a chunk out of the pot and put it in our mouth, we have no idea what it now will taste like until it hits our taste buds. My daughter, who could be psychic I suppose, thinks she can still recognize something in that stew that she calls carrots, without putting them in her mouth. She picks out these little orange chunks and asks, "Do I have to eat the carrots?" Now, I used to help my father grow carrots in our garden. So I know that carrots are long and skinny and bright orange, and when you grab the big furry green top, pull it up out of the ground, rub the dirt off on your pants, and chomp down, they're actually pretty tasty. But as everyone knows, the most distinguishing characteristic of a carrot is the "Crunch".

What makes my daughter think this pale orange chunk in the stew that mushes in your mouth is a carrot? Her perception comes from her past experience, the fun in pushing parental mealtime limits, and her creative imagination. This ingredient in the stew is not long and tapered. It is small and angular. The only similarity to a carrot is the somewhat orange color, now burnished with a dripping brown coating. It does not taste like the carrot you pull from the ground. And it most definitely does not crunch. It is nothing like a real carrot, but her mind and memory fill in the missing form, crunch, length, and flavor (which is now definitely beef bullion).

Perhaps this kind of experience may be similar to how some people encounter dead souls. When these experiences happen, dead people are not usually encountered as complete beings in physical bodies. But perhaps we humans can sometimes fill in the voids from our past experience, knowledge, emotion, imagination, and intuitive senses. Things that jog our memory, touch our emotions, or bits of information we pick up in every day activities or with extra sensory perception can quickly be filled in with human form or former characteristics. There is no way my daughter will ever believe that what was in the beef stew was an orange colored piece of tofu. To my daughter it will always be carrot. To some people who encounter bits of information or unconscious perception from their own or other people's memory bank, it is easy to believe this is a communication with dear departed Uncle Fred.

In Conjuring Up Philip Iris Owen described a carefully controlled project that showed how this encounter with dead souls and spirits is a real experience, but probably the projection of our own minds. Some people can go into trance and talk with a different voice, personality, or through the personality of a "spirit guide". There is no question that many of these mediums are charlatans and use illusion and vague verbal slight of hand to create what appears to be telepathic or psychokinetic experiences. But sometimes psychics relay detail or personal information that is totally astounding to those who seek them out, and there is no question in their minds that something is taking place beyond usual sensory and communication levels. The encounter with the spirit entity of Philip, however, came from the gathering of a group of people experienced in psychic phenomena, in a controlled environment, with cameras recording the events. This group was asked first to deliberately make up a story of a ghost named Philip. Collectively they strung together a story of a noble who lived during the reign of King Charles. He fell in love with a young girl. His wife falsely accused the girl of witchcraft and she was sentenced to death because Philip refused to defend her. Instead he chose to kill himself. Although the tale was completely the fabrication of this group of eight, they then began conducting a seance around a table to try to communicate with the spirit of Philip. They waited for recognized signs and sounds of spirit communication, such as the table tilting or producing rapping sounds, in response to questions they asked about

Philip. The entire story of Philip's sad life was conveyed back to the group through the rapping signals from the table in a séance with the "spirit of Philip".

Numerous reports of telepathic, psychokinetic, and near death experiences are evidence that we occasionally have the ability (some people more than others) to transcend our normal ways of knowing, experiencing, and encountering reality. But as this experiment shows, this does not necessarily lead to the conclusion that there actually are other spirit entities beyond our own fertile mental abilities. Some people seem to have a limited ability to project or detect some knowledge and awareness non-verbally across space. Dreams and intuitions sometimes reveal anticipation of future events, especially in twins, although more commonly our dream events obviously never happen. Our consciousness functions primarily in our everyday sensory world, but has limited abilities in amazing and astounding ways occasionally to experience some things apparently beyond our normal perceptions of space and time.

If we intuit bits and pieces of knowledge, feeling, or perception that exist in the consciousness of others, we interpret it in the only ways we can. We fill in the meaning from our own memory and knowledge even to the point where it feels as though we are communicating with another human like being. The stuff in the stew will always be a carrot to my daughter and to some people their encounter with an altered state of consciousness will always be a very real encounter with Jesus, a spirit guide, or Uncle Fred even though another person in the same circumstances will have a different experience or detect nothing at all.

The near death experience (NDE) that some people report is another example of how altered states of consciousness can lead to an interpretation of the existence of non-physical spiritual entities. In near death experiences people are not just unconscious. Physical functioning to support life has stopped. Not everyone who dies or almost dies and then is resuscitated reports these experiences, of course. When they have occurred, however, there tend to be some common images and sensations that people report: a sense of being dead, peacefulness and painlessness, moving through a long tunnel, a review of life events, a reluctance to return to their body and their material life, or an encounter with friendly non-material beings who are either recognized or unknown. Some report the most important part of a NDE is an encounter with a central core of light associated with a feeling of infinite love and peacefulness, that if they go toward, they will not return to their body. It is this latter encounter that people often cite as having a transforming effect on them and their lives after they come back to life. (Melvin Morse. Transformed by the Light.)

As the ability of a human body to maintain life starts to fade and becomes disorganized, what many have called the soul leaving the body, rather than an expected panicky feeling, people with NDE often report an awareness of peaceful belonging and acceptance. Melvin Morse, M.D., who has studied this phenomenon at length, concludes that this experience is one which takes place in the right temporal lobe of the brain. Dr. Andrew Newberg at the University of Pennsylvania and others have shown that suppression of the superior parietal lobes of the brain produces a break-down of the mind's ability to distinguish between itself and the outside world. This loss of the ability to identify oneself as separate creates an experience of joining with the infinite. With electrical stimulation neurosurgeons during awake brain surgery have been able to cause people out of body and other mystical experiences. All the elements reported in near death experiences have been duplicated by brain stimulation, except Morse claims, the encounter with the Great White Light. He believes that when the cells begin to die and genetic DNA material releases the energy of its organizational power and life force, electromagnetic energy is given off that either stimulates the right temporal lobe or is detected by it. Morse calls this part of the brain, "the seat of the soul". All of this information suggests that all our various mystical experiences of the Infinite are based on the anatomical workings of our brain.

Bob told me his personal experience of dying. His car flipped over into a pond, landing upside down, crushing the top, leaving him trapped upside down. He couldn't release his jammed seat belt as the water rose inside the car. He suffered a slow, terrifying death as he repeatedly breathed in water, and then each time, trying not to breath for a little bit longer. He remembers eventually getting light headed and passing out, and then from somewhere above his overturned car, observing his body being retrieved by policemen. He watched the unsuccessful resuscitation attempt by the police and EMTs. He floated along just above the ambulance to the emergency room and watched his lungs being suctioned out and his body shocked in an attempt to restart his heart. From a comfortable spot up near the clock on the wall he observed his family come to visit his lifeless body in the hospital room. An unrecognizable but definite personality joined him up by the clock saying that he had a choice of remaining in this safe comfortable dimension where he now was, but that he also had the choice and was encouraged to return to his wife and family because this had been an accident and his family still needed him.

These experiences are just as real to people who have them as getting a hamburger at McDonalds, but its effect is usually longer lasting and much more profound. Many of those who experience a NDE usually report no more fear of death though some find the experience terrifying. They tend to believe that our molecules will pass away, as will our individuality, but that our individual manifestation of soul will return to the one Soul from which everything came and that it is a good experience. This experience and interpretation may be based on a purely materially caused brain event at the time of dying, but it is remembered as a spiritual and emotional experience. This dramatic experience of our awareness of our connection with the Infinite, this perception triggered by our cells dying and organized life disintegrating in our body does not prove that there is an individual non-material existence for human souls after our bodies die. We are obviously not able to ask people who stay dead what their experience is after the experience of dying. Is that because there is no individual soul without physical existence? NDE is certainly a dramatic, curious, and sometimes reassuring experience for those who encounter it, but it raises more questions than it provides explanations.

Most people seem to assume that if souls exist independently from bodies, that they leave when the body stops breathing, but the issue of afterlife is as speculative as before life. If there are non-material, infinite beings then they can exist anywhere, anytime, in fact must exist without time. Popular wisdom doesn't usually address where all these souls might be before they're born, or whether they come into existence only every time another human is conceived. Do souls line up to get a body, like waiting to get into a rock concert or a playoff game; or do they have a lottery? This speculation sounds odd because we focus more on when the soul might leave the body than when it enters. This is because we struggle more emotionally with our death than we do with our birth. It seems likely that what we call our individual soul is our inherited portion of the Unifying Force of all Creation that provides continuity, cohesion, and organization to all the cells of our body as well as our mind, and that it begins to evolve with conception, deteriorates with aging, and ends with death.

When we lose this underlying, unconscious unifying and organizing force at the cellular level, our body dies. When we lose our conscious unifying and organizing force, we lose our personality. If we lose either our cellular identity or our conscious personality, we lose what we would call our individual soul. Anyone who has watched a loved one's personality change after a permanent brain injury or Alzheimer's disease, has watched a personality and a soul die before the body does. What is it that is left in these bodies? Is there a soul in there? If there is a soul remaining, either soul has no identifiable permanent personality since this is clearly not the same person as before; soul is only some organizing force of the material body that keeps it breathing but has no personality; or this person's soul has already left this material body along with their old personality. We still love and honor the person who used to spring forth from this body by taking care of the body, but the person we loved is gone. Anyone who has ever lost a loved one before their body dies, may conclude that the individual soul and personality of each person are inseparable, that the individuality of each disappear together. Emotionally we want to act as though the person we loved is still in that body, just hidden from view; but over months and sometimes even years, most family members come to the conclusion that this is not the person they used to know and love. We want to hope that their personality and soul is still in there somewhere. Experience is showing us that they're not there any more.

My brother-in-law eventually not only could not function as the aggressive trial lawyer he had been, he eventually could not reliably find his way home when he took a walk after Alzheimer's debilitated him in his late fifties. He lost his memory, his ability to process new information, and to care for himself. Whatever was still living was not what was there before. As family we felt we slowly lost him long before his body ceased to breathe. We grieved both times, but in the end it was also a relief that he got cancer and his body stopped. Anything that we celebrate and fondly remember as the essence of him was gone long before. If what left when he stopped breathing was his spirit, then spirit doesn't contain much for human beings to relate to. The essence of him that we loved resides satisfyingly in our hearts, but it was not in his body for a long time before it died. Our most individualistic expression and manifestation of the Eternal Life-Giving Soul is our human personality. Together our soul and personality bloom and together they merge back into the Cosmic Ground from which being springs forth again, ashes to ashes, dust to dust, molecule to molecule, millennium to millennium.

So with what do we communicate when some humans have an occasional experience of encountering a non-material being, ghost, or spirit? The existence of individual spirits separate from an alive body, a personality that is a spirit beyond the Spirit that is in everything, appears to be an outreach of our own mind onto the Eternal All and the Great Unknown. We encounter non-material personalities, angels, and aliens as well as our own souls through the projection of our mind's personality and perception. It is inevitable that we think of the Great Spirit that infuses our life to have some human like characteristics also, because our most sophisticated thoughts, deepest emotions, and most reverent speculations come from a human mind. It is from this same difficulty to imagine creation coming from any other perspective than a human like mind that we imagine the continuity of our spirit after death can only be as a human personality.

Overcoming the Fear of Death

There is no evidence that human like consciousness and personality can exist without a centralizing material core such as a live brain. Information itself does exist in the universe independent of human consciousness, the kind of information, for instance, that allows cells to divide and reproduce themselves or the information that governs gravity. Life associated with our distinct recognizable personality, however, is supported only by our human material bodies, and afterlife is supported primarily by the projection of our emotional needs and human like qualities onto the unknown. What is probably most important about afterlife is not whether it exists or not, but the fact that it really doesn't matter very much. It simply is not important to most people, most of the days of their lives, whether they're really dead when they die. What is more important is how we live.

Except for the few willing to die based on their belief that today's behavior is going to determine their future rewards, belief in before or afterlife really doesn't have much impact on our everyday lives. The joyful fact is, however, that we don't need a belief in future rewards or punishments nor in the existence of souls without bodies to live a full, thoughtful, caring, and spiritual life. We choose religious and secular beliefs that best support the emotional and intellectual needs of our current stage of personality development and life circumstances. Depressed people who never go to church and couldn't tell a crucifix from a stick of incense will sometimes still say they won't commit suicide for fear of going to Hell—and they don't even really believe in Hell. What they probably feel is a desire to continue living and a great respect for the sacredness of life. Most people tend to use edited religious doctrine, selected scriptures, and carefully screened religious beliefs to support whatever they already believe or what seems to address their current problems and life issues. It is not surprising that most people do not think about religious issues every day and don't guide their daily decision making by anything having to do with an afterlife, fear of going to Hell, reward in Heaven, or the possible non-existence of their soul after death.

The lack of belief in an after-life or disembodied souls does not necessarily reduce our interest in spirituality, however. In fact removing non-worldly mythology focuses a greater importance on everyday, down-to-earth spirituality. If the reason for living this life is to get on to another one, we'd probably all be better off punching fast forward. But some people really treasure their lifetime and so they do not fear death and emotionally embrace it when it is time. My father was one. He literally gave his life to the church. He was a loving and gentle man who in his twenties was called back to Indiana from his horse riding circuit, preaching in rural churches in Montana, where he had gone to live until his severe diabetes would end his life. Luckily, Eli Lilly Corporation was in Indiana and the locals knew about their recently discovered ability to manufacture insulin. So they called him back, he gave himself shots twice a day for the next forty years, got married, raised a family, continued his ministry, lived until he was 65, and his essence continues on in me.

The last 10 years of his life the effects of his diabetes caused a heart attack and eventually some of his intellectual sharpness began to slip. So he took a lessor position as an assistant pastor at a large church in the big city. It was a good move, made possible by the strength of humility. It went well until a new senior pastor was appointed who turned out to be a general rogue who was stealing from the church. My father discovered this and tried to talk with him on a personal basis but eventually felt compelled to announce at the church board meeting that he could not continue working with this senior pastor. The Bishop, the big boss, and a good friend of our family, rather than support his longtime friend, chastised my father's complaints as insubordination, acting "out of character", and not keeping the peace. There was nothing for my father to do but to resign from the one thing he loved and still did very well: minister to people's spiritual needs. Our family spent the several months before he could retire and claim social security encouraging my father to take up hobbies, plant a bigger garden, fussing over his future. He said not to worry. Things would work out.

Shortly after retiring he and my mother went on a trip to visit her sister on the East Coast. While on this visit, he became ill and died there in a matter of a few hours. I like to think he not only unconsciously planned when but also where he was going to die, where he would not unduly burden his children, where my mother would be embraced and comforted. I am quite certain he died at this time because his reason for living was finished, his life complete, true to the end to himself and his values, accepting and loving of not only his bishop friend who did not believe him, but forgiving the bastard (O.K., so I've also got some of my mother's essence in me also who knew for sure this guy was going to burn in Hell) whom they eventually caught and threw out of the church.

My father's severe diabetes was wicked, with many nights of my youth struggling awake to massage his cramping legs and forcing sugar laced orange juice through his clenched teeth while he hallucinated or was incoherent. I always thought of it as his "Going to Missouri" after one of his more riotous and frightening insulin reaction induced hallucinations. And then he would get up the next morning and tend to his flock or preach from the pulpit. He could have died as a young man, or during multiple low blood sugar crises and insulin reactions, or during his heart attack. At the time of his death my father's day to day health was the best it had been in several years, but he died when his reason for living was done. I was sad for me but happy for him. What could be better than to live a long life, clear about what's important, faithful in your commitments, helping some people along the way, and dying when you're done?

Interestingly, my mother also apparently chose when to die. Some years after my father's death she developed lupus which eventually destroyed her kidneys, and wasn't so kind to some of her joints and other organs. Her life-long personality and determination was never to be dependent on anyone. She vowed never to live with her children in order not to interfere with their lives. She had a retirement home picked out, but I think it was just a story to keep her kids from fussing over her. This active energetic person simply felt lousy for several years and pushed her body around from sheer will. She would go to work Monday, Wednesday and Friday and go to the hospital for hours of kidney dialysis on Tuesday, Thursday, and Saturday. This went on for a few years with a couple of hospitalizations when the lupus acted worse and the reassuring visit to Mayo Clinic to learn that her local doctors were doing all they could. So, she went on. Go to work. Go to dialysis. Have the grandkids over. And then one weekend she went in the hospital and died. I think she chose to die then because she couldn't live her way any more. She too was able to be faithful to herself and her values throughout her life, and when she couldn't do it any more, she died.

Unfortunately not all of us will get to die quickly or when we choose too. With modern science, more of us will die of old age, slow degenerating deaths. In fact we have learned that doctors and hospitals are good at keeping us alive longer, but they are generally not as good at helping us die gracefully. In fact the medical system sometimes complicates the process or gets in the way. The continuing waves of legislation reclaiming patient rights not to be kept alive against their will have been necessary to protect us from doctors and hospitals who deal with their own pain and suffering about death by resisting letting patients die, or who put the fear of lawsuits ahead of withholding futile treatments. There are potential legal threats, moral rationalizations, family and physician pain, and medical single mindedness that sometimes pressure to sustain life even when patients don't want it, or encourage futile treatment that only prolongs dying rather than preventing death. Most "codes" in hospitals and most of our health care dollars are used in the last six months of people's lives. Only 40 percent of all cardiac resuscitations in hospitals, the famous "codes" of TV hospital show fame, are successful. Only half of those who are resuscitated ever leave the hospital alive, "saved" by a bone breaking procedure that was meant for street use, not for hospital patients. Living a little longer is not how we can overcome our fear of death. Living a little more fully and thoughtfully is how we do that. Planning our own death and memorial service when life is clearly no longer an option is a sacred honor. When our society is less afraid of death and more truly reverent of life, we will more clearly support people's choices about when and how they finally die.

A man came to my office saying he now understood why his father "gave up" and died after a history of heart disease. Because he now has the same illness, he feels the frustration and fatigue of dealing with pain every day, an uncertain future, and fear of losing control of acceptable levels of personal functioning. He knows he is living to see his son graduate and get married and that goal will keep his fears and fatigue at bay at the moment. He'll stay alive, in spite of doctors expecting him to be dead five years ago based on his medical tests, double digit heart surgeries and daily super-size doses of nitroglycerin. Oh, he'll most likely die of heart disease or something related to it; but he's not going to die just yet, and the primary reason is that he's busy living the way he wants to. He is not afraid to live his life, in spite of the fact that he is more aware than most of us that his days are numbered. There have been many scary nights for him and his sons—both fearing that the sunrise would find him dead. But he goes to work everyday, takes trips across the country to visit his family, is active in religious and social events, exercises at the rehab center, and entertained the possibility of starting a new career in another state—in spite of the very real possibility that he could be dead tomorrow. He's doing the important things in his life now, not putting them off, not being afraid something will happen if he takes a chance, not waiting for another chance. The illness has become a blessing as well as a threat. He now lives by the motto:

Live as though you'll die tomorrow.

Plan was though you'll live forever.

We can deliberately and consciously express God through us by how we live, or our lives can just be a part of the mass necessary to sustain human existence. It is a pretty amazing opportunity that we even have some choice about the nature of our existence. We may only be like a drop of water that falls onto a vast ocean, making small circles on the surface that slowly move outward in ever increasing halos, the single drop no longer identified but becoming part of a larger body of water whose molecules are being slowly evaporated and elevated by the heat of the sun to blow with the winds across a continent, to reform in a cloud where a new droplet of water falls in the stream from which the young drink to sustain new life. Our single identity may not last forever, but each life shapes and brings forth the future. It is choice that makes humans really special. We make big choices and little ones and together they are our statement about why life, not death is the defining part of our existence.

In both beliefs and actions we need less emphasis on trying to prevent the inevitability of death or fantasizing that it isn't really final, and more emphasis on how we live. Death is part of the innate gift of life and clarifies the importance of how we live each and every day. Creation sustains itself through a finite series of events that unfold to the next, including human life. No individual is eternal, but is part of Eternity. We are not immortal but we are the highest expression of God on this Earth. Let us celebrate both our individual existence and our common source. Let us deliberately enhance life and bring honor to our opportunity to be the voice and conscience of God on Earth. The legacy we leave for the next generation and the next into millenniums is our afterlife. Let us not worry about our mortality but rather celebrate our living, accepting both that we have made a difference and perhaps could have done more, but have done our part.

> It is not finished, Lord.
> There is not one thing done.
> There is no battle of my life that I have really won.
> And now I come to tell Thee how I ought to fall.
> My human, all too human tale of weakness and futility,
> And yet there is a faith in me that Thou will find in it
> One word that Thou canst take, and make
> The center of a sentence in Thy book of poetry.

I cannot read the writing of the years,
My eyes are full of tears—it gets all blurred
And won't make sense.
Its full of contradictions like the scribblings of a child.

Such wild, wild hopes and longings as intense as pain
Which trivial deeds make folly of—or worse:

I can but hand it in, and hope that They great Mind
Which reads the writings of so many lives
Will understand this scrawl
And what it strives to say
But leaves unsaid.

I cannot write it over,
The stars are coming out,
My body needs its bed.

I have no strength for more,
So it must stand or fall,
Dear Lord,

That's all!

Studdard Kennedy

Figuring Out How to Live

> In the end, there must be a purpose to our journey. Human endeavor cannot consist simply of random acts and happenstance. There needs to be meaning beyond self that gives our limited days definition and direction. And only within that meaning can the judgment rendered upon our lives have worth. (Paul Tsongas. Journey of Purpose.)

By the time I was in high school I had perfected acting perfect. I did the right things, mostly out of fear of failure, but everybody's parents loved me. I didn't swear. Didn't drink alcohol. Didn't use drugs. Was on the basketball team. (In Indiana that was better than being an alter boy.) Because my father was a minister I got points for that too. Nobody liked running track, so I was pretty good there too. I got all A's in school. I could speak well before groups, probably from watching may father in the pulpit every Sunday forever. (Can you believe we even went to church when we were on vacation?) Now, he really was a good man. I, of course, was just pretending. In 7th grade I once thought I'd practice a little swearing. Where better to try out something you're a little unsure of than with your mother? It seemed like a pretty good idea to me until her full round house slap sent me halfway across the room. She had never hit me like that! I thought this must be a case of mistaken identity. It was. I had momentarily forgotten who I was supposed to be. So you can see with all these influences, it was much easier just to become perfect than to become normal. Simply by doing what other people wanted and said was good, I found I could gain acceptance, social approval, direction for life, the promise of immortality in Eternity—and most important of all, not get a girl pregnant.

Fortunately, I lived long enough to grow up, to become something more than a follower of the rules and brave enough to start engaging life instead of trying to leap from one pedestal to another. Life becomes so much richer, interesting and exciting when we're not terrified of making a mistake. After we have proven we can follow rules and behave responsibly, the next level of moral and spiritual growth is to make our own choices about how we are going to act, what we believe and how we will commit our life energies.

The biggest problem with trying to do the right thing is the impossibility of knowing for sure what is Right. We do all sorts of things to deal with this dilemma. Some declare that they have the right interpretation or the only true revelation. Some try to pacify their uncertainty and fear by judging or attacking people who have a different set of value beliefs. Banding together against some common opponent or enemy can identify where we belong and clarify our purpose. Some people band together to save owls, others to save the planet, or to save themselves. Other people belong to a group who take pride in doing their job well, working longer, harder, or accumulating things. Some gain money or influence to verify their worth. Some people just stay busy, so they don't have to think about whether what they are doing is worthwhile or has any meaning. Our lives "require some assembly" and in fact there is no one right way it will go together. A spiritual person tries to assemble their life with thoughtfulness and purpose.

Our faithful dog Pooh Bear was part of our family for 17 years until we had the vet put him to sleep one Spring. He was a typical dig in the flowers, jump on your good clothes, lick your face, get in the garbage, love-you-forever mutt. But he also got old. His night vision went, so unhappily he did his yard business closer and closer to the front door. The cataracts took away a good portion of his day vision as well. So when we opened the door to his beckoning whine to be let in, he couldn't find the opening, though he was standing right in front of the door. Like every long eared dog I've had, he also became deaf, except if you clapped your hand's together loudly from within ten feet. Communication was mostly jumping up and down on the floor and arm waving to get his attention, grateful that he learned some sign language. He had great difficulty getting to a standing position except during his nightly burst of energy between 5 and 7 PM. Then when he did totter all the way to his feet, we immediately chased him outdoors because he had lost most of his bowel and bladder control. All this was complicated, of course, by the Alzheimer's. When he thought he wanted to go outside, he often stood in front of the grandfather clock, thinking it was the door (or perhaps he was just a deeply wise dog into symbolism). But we could live with all this, and did for a growing number of years, delaying replacing the soiled carpet, because we loved him, or more accurately, we didn't want to let go of our love for him, and wanted to honor and cherish the love he had brought to our family.

What became the most difficult to ignore was his misery. When he did get to his feet, he could only stand with his head hanging nearly to the floor, in too much pain to move even one step, but also clearly not wanting to move. He didn't want to go anywhere, not even sure where "there" was any more. He no longer understood that being petted or even touched was intended as an act of love. This just added to his annoyance and increased his groans of misery. There was clearly no more purpose, no enjoyment, only struggle. Like many of us, who will be kept from the swifter killing diseases of the past, he died in small increments over a very long time.

How does one act morally in this situation? How does one try to carry out a chosen goal to make more good happen in the world than bad? What actions reflect a commitment to act in loving ways? We were willing to continue cleaning up the diarrhea and vomit all over the house, but it really seemed more loving to "put him to sleep"—our attempt to mask the decision to kill our dog. The morally right thing to do was to keep following the values, making caring and thoughtful choices, not so much which choices were made. This is where we earn in anguish and tears this wonderful opportunity to decide for ourselves how we will live our lives, having to decide and commit to an action, especially when it includes both good and bad, joy and pain, celebration and grief all at the same time. But it is in these moments of decision and commitment that we express both our fullest humanity and our fullest divinity. The human price for evolving to such a highly complex level of development is not only more ability to choose, but also to feel the moral responsibility and sometimes the pain of our decisions.

Should we give powerful drugs to people who are in physical or emotional pain, even though it might hasten their death? Should we give up a child for adoption or abort the fetus because we cannot care for the child? Very loving, caring and spiritual people differ over these questions. Being moral is not a matter of doing the right thing. It is a matter of making decisions and acting without always knowing for sure whether we are right, but committing ourselves to living up to the highest and best we can, accepting the responsibility, the outcomes, and our own doubts. Following rules is not the same as acting morally; it's just the beginning. Choosing a set of values and principles to live by, making the most important decisions of our lives based on those values, and then accepting that we have done our best—that's what make's our lives both sacred and morally strong. Life is ours to spend anyway we chose. It's challenging! It's precious! It's the highest expression of Creation on our Earth!

Using What We Can from Religious Traditions

Some feel guided in their life course and moral deliberations by aligning themselves with the past, to the things that haven't changed in hundreds or thousands of years: to the Torah, the Koran, the Bible, the Veda, or the I'Ching. Some feel guided by their social roots and history: Moses in Egypt, through the Diaspora and the Holocaust, up to Joseph's Bar Mitzvah on Saturday—all giving continuity and connection. The Orthodox Whatever Religion offers direction by presenting teachings and rules to live by that previous faithful followers endorsed. Mystics of all religious persuasions may ignore what has gone before and rediscover for the first time their inspiration directly from God, through prayer, meditation, or chakra connections with the spiritual plane. The Dali Lama has spoken thoughtfully of this: If you were born into a Buddhist culture, be the best Buddhist you can be. If your were born into a Muslim culture, be the best Muslim you can be. If you were born into a Catholic home, be the best Catholic you can be. If we all have this common commitment, hopefully our common values will overcome our intellectual and religious differences and bring us together.

Some religions invite people to obtain assurance of their worth and place in the universe by confessing misdeeds and experiencing the relief that brings with feelings of forgiveness, acceptance, and love. This can be a purifying and refocusing experience, but for many it becomes a meaningless ritual. This is sometimes mixed in with an old fashioned dose of a wrathful god, with the threat that if we don't heed this particular invitation to accept their brand of forgiveness, there are some pretty bad things in store for us. The idea that we are accepted by Creation and the Source of All Being only if we accept a particular religious doctrine or means of encountering God portrays God just as petty and narrow minded as we humans can be—hardly a very lofty concept. If there really is a unified life-giving force, all powerful and nurturing, then embracing any particular sanctioned understanding or doctrine is not the only way to Heaven, Nirvana, or personal salvation. The Christian theological notion that an all powerful God sacrificed his only son to show that we are loved in spite of our (may we be so bold as to say "small") faults and indiscretions, is a powerful message, encased in an ancient sacrificial myth, in order to get to the bottom line. It seems less complicated and more inclusive, more God like, to say that all people are equal sons and daughters of Creation, and that Jesus, Mohammed, Buddha, Lao Tse, and all the rest of us are equally precious manifestations of God.

The powerful concept of New Testament writings, and the reason that I am a Christian atheist, is that no matter how badly we have prioritized our lives, how many mistakes we have made, how many people we have hurt, how much we have just wandered around aimlessly with our lives, the Universe equally accepts and values us anyway. If we endorse this concept, then God embraces all people, no matter their theology or whether they even believe in or have any experience of a unifying Spirit or not. As part of All Creation, we belong here on this Earth, on this planet, in this galaxy, in this universe, each of us deserving of respect and recognition of our small but unique role. This is a profoundly liberating personal message of self-acceptance. It doesn't matter how we look, what we think, how we worship, or how we act. All are equally valued and are expressions of God, the atoms of your body, the longings of your heart, and the thoughts of your mind equally precious expressions of the Universe as are mine and everyone else's.

In Heaven's eyes
There are no losers…
No hopeless cause
Only people like you
With feelings like me
Amazed by the grace we can find….

("In Heaven's Eyes". Words
and music by Phill McHugh.)

Our knowledge of how things work no longer allows us to think of God as a puppeteer pulling the strings of our every day existence, but we still emotionally and spiritually wish for someone in charge, someone who can verify that we are special, or at least care about how we live and what we do. It may be asking a bit much, but we'd even like to feel that someone up there loved us, kind of like the Big Mother of the Sky. Our emotional needs were met very nicely by some traditional religious concepts and mythologies even though the intellectual validity of that framework is no longer viable; but that doesn't mean there is no love in creation any more. Love, meaning, and purpose are all available to us. There is someone to declare that we are special, that it makes a difference how we live. It's just that it's down here, not up there; in here, not out there; today, not tomorrow.

I grew up with a personal relationship with God. I talked to God regularly and experienced an intense, warm feeling inside, a presence of a caring imaginary father/mother personality who was close to me whenever I closed my eyes and focused intensely on the feeling. A feeling that brought tears to my eyes. A feeling that uplifted me. A mystical connection with God that immediately gave comfort and emotional strength. After I learned more about science and studied theology, as much as I might want to, I couldn't believe in that kind of God any more. Guess what? I still get teary-eyed, am easily touched by warm and intense emotions, get inspired, and live thoughtfully. I even have brief conversations with God sometimes because it's a familiar and convenient way to focus my thoughts, calm my emotions, and transcend my immediate emotional state, although I am more likely to pursue those activities in mindful meditation.

Many religious people engage in similar activities and experiences and interpret them as being in the presence of God or experiencing the Holy Spirit. These are sometimes strongly emotional experiences, the rational meaning or source of which are not questioned. The sense that we are not controlled by or at the mercy of our fears and struggles is an amazingly powerful experience. It doesn't matter whether this reassurance is interpreted as coming from the presence of a supreme being or simply an experience of deep inner peacefulness from within us. We feel better, calmer, more joyful, more peaceful, more confident, and more content. These personal experiences of holy intensity have repeatedly renewed the lives of people with weary spirits and sometimes revealed direction and purpose to those who were drifting. Many people, however, don't have these experiences but still want a framework to direct their lives. The attempt in these pages to understand how science and human consciousness and our place in the universe all tie together without traditional religious beliefs and mythologies hopefully will be of use to some.

Ritual, ceremonial worship, meditation, and music also help create a personal feeling of upliftment and common high purpose. We can increase the inspirational potential of religious ceremonies and practices if we replace or at least supplement traditional religious ceremony and ritual with new forms and expressions. There is a big difference in my mood and probably in the cells of my body when listening to droning church hymns on a pipe organ than when listening to the driving base guitar, drums, and keyboard of a can't-keep-my-foot from tapping rhythm. Clearly the latter moves my spirit more. It doesn't matter what the words are. The language and the message is the music itself. Clapping, dancing and singing are as enlivening, energizing, and uplifting for us as it was for the Psalmists who heard a different but equally spiritual rhythm and danced to different drums.

> Praise the Lord!...Praise him with trumpet sound; praise him with lute and harp!
> Praise him with timbrel and dance; praise him with strings and pipe!
> Praise him with sounding cymbals; praise him with loud clashing cymbals!
> Let everything that breathes praise the Lord!...
> (Psalms 150)

In order to have a fuller, more meaningful, and less schizophrenic spirituality, whatever we say in worship or on a poetic, emotional, or spiritual level, must also integrate with what we know on a scientific and everyday factual level. There is a very good possibility that we came into existence by chance or accident, that both the Big Bang and all creation might be a mistake or a malfunction of perfect unity. But just because birth control sometimes doesn't work and pregnancies are sometimes unplanned does not mean that the off-spring are unloving or unloved. Just because we might be an unplanned surprise in the Universe doesn't mean that we should stop celebrating the wonder of our creation, sometimes with the same words as our ancestors:

> For the beauty of the earth
> For the glory of the skies
> For the love which from our birth
> Over and around us lies:
> For the beauty of each hour
> Of the day and of the night
> Hill and vale and tree and flower
> Sun and moon and stars of light
> For the joy of ear and eye
> For the heart and mind's delight
> For the mystic harmony
> Linking sense to sound and sight
> Lord of all to Thee we raise
> This our hymn of grateful praise.
>
> ("For the Beauty of the Earth"
> Folliot S. Pierpoint, 1864.
> <u>Methodist Hymnal</u>)

Building Our Own Spiritual Foundation

There are several building blocks that can help us form our own spiritual foundation:

1. Fearless acceptance of our finiteness and gratitude for the opportunity to be here.
2. Building relationships with others to reduce the loneliness of our individual existence.
3. Nurturing our ability to directly experience our connection to the Universe.
4. Creating direction and meaning by living purposefully.

The **first** ingredient for transcending the otherwise somewhat frightening realization of our finiteness is developing an appreciation and gratefulness for the opportunity just to be here. It helps us with the disappointment that we won't be forever. We don't have to interpret this reality as depressing. The realization that we can make choices and shape not only our own lives but also the next generation and the future of the Universe is an amazing and wonderful gift! Hoping that an afterlife will be the reward for how we lived this one suggests that perhaps we aren't treating today with enough reverence. To express our free will is our opportunity. To make choices is our responsibility. To have this one life is our gift.

Especially when life is hard or boring, we wish that Someone or Something would tell us how to live, cast a long shadow over our freedom, assure us that it's all worth it or that there is a larger purpose. We can transcend the limitations of our existence, but it takes a daily appreciation of the precious gift of our existence. Larry Dossey quotes a Buddhist philosopher as saying:

> Before Enlightenment,
> Carry water, chop wood.
> After Enlightenment,
> Carry water, chop wood.

Life is transformed only by the attitude we adopt, transforming it from simple drudgery or a fear filled test into a divine expression.

A **second** spiritual ingredient that turns the separation of our existence from fear and isolation into comfort and joy is that we can build relationships during our life that fill our need to renew our connectedness. Love is the emotional solution to the loneliness of our separate, physical existence. The easiest way that we can feel connected is to give love to someone else. Some of us wait around for someone to love us and feel the world is unfair or uncaring when we don't get as much as we need. But addressing our own emotional need for love is very simple. In giving love and caring for someone else, we experience love ourselves. We can overcome our own isolation and feeling of separation by reaching out to the needs of others. When we extend our hand to comfort someone else, we experience the comfort the Universe has for everyone. When we give love, we feel the Universe embrace us as well.

Churches, synagogues, temples and mosques are the gathering places where we can join to recognize our common source and to join with others who chose to live intentionally. Not everyone is going to understand or celebrate their spirituality in the same way. My perfect church would be 15 minutes of Quaker silence, 15 minutes of a demythologized preacher who tells inspirational stories in current life, coupled with 20 minutes of a good band and a gospel choir. My mind yearns for the intellectual stimulation of spiritual reflection and the emotional inspiration that come from stories of the goodness of our spiritual brothers and sisters; but my soul wants the enthusiasm and vibrational energy of the rhythms. My feet start tapping and my soul starts moving when James Brown starts shouting Eeeeeeeoooooow! It really doesn't matter whether the words are "Praise the Lord, Oh My Soul" or "I've Got Twenty More Pancakes to Fry". Fortunately a few worship services are now emerging that cross church denominational lines and bring together down to earth theology with up to the sky music, videos, humor, and drama that address spirituality in every day life and give people somewhere to gather who can't relate to traditional religious worship.

A **third** opportunity that increases spiritual vitality is to directly experience being connected to the Universe. A personal relationship with a human-like god figure is not the only way of directly experiencing spiritual connection, however. Mysticism comes in both religious and secular forms. Some people pray. Some go into trance or meditative states in which they experience an amorphous Oneness or simply a deep sense of inner peace and calm that drives out fear and isolation. Others sing, chant, or exercise their way into transcendent feeling. Some have found this experience with the aid of chemicals or plants or fasting. Perhaps in the future we may seek spiritual awareness with electrical brain stimulation. Others quietly mediate or contemplate the beauty of Nature or the vastness of the stars.

Meditative silence produces transcendent calm that overcomes our isolation and fear. One simple way to experience inner peace is to be completely physically and mentally still. Dr. Craig Overmeyer, a pastoral counselor and life coach, has beautifully interpreted this passage from Psalm 46:10 in Dynamic Health (Insight Publications):

> Be still and know that I am God.
>
> Be still and know that I am.
>
> Be still and know.
>
> Be still.
>
> Be.

Separate from our rational thinking, separate from our relationships with others, separate from our symbolic and mythological imagery, we have a way of experiencing the Infinite that is direct and immediate. It is unmediated by organized religion, priests, or doctrine. We have only to be still, to sense it. Human consciousness is an outgrowth of the matter of creation. We can become aware of our connection to God, to Everything, simply by quieting the noise our mind makes. Both our physical and emotional hearts are the creation and evolution of the One. Bringing this awareness into our consciousness, "bringing God into our hearts", is simply a matter of being emotionally and intellectually quiet enough to feel our spiritual roots.

A **fourth** opportunity to create a strong spiritual foundation is to live purposefully. What we do is not as critical as the fact that our commitments give our lives purpose. Becoming president of something is no more important to our spiritual vitality than coming home on time to let the dog out or take the kids to soccer practice. It is our commitments that define our lives, create our purpose, and apply our spiritual understanding. This is not the same as being busy. Sometimes we fill up our lives with so many events and demands that we are overwhelmed and can't possibly live thoughtfully. Sometime we stay busy not because we have to but because we try to substitute activity for purpose, fatigue for meaning, and busyness for love. But our feelings of isolation and estrangement only get worse if we don't intentionally create love and purpose with our lives and simply allow birth and death to define our existence. We build the meaning of our existence and demonstrate our spiritual development with each deed, each day, each moment.

Divinity has always occurred in those who take the time to embrace their spirituality and incorporate their values into intentional living. Our spirituality is like the bloom of a flower that projects a basic shape and color. But we can notice more. We can notice the fragrance, a very faint but distinct smell, sharp but pleasant. Then we notice that the beauty of the deep rich red is magnified by the dark green leaves. We want to touch those petals. They have the multiple sensations of velvet. We feel uplifted, enjoying not only this single flower but all the memories and associations it stirs, including the happy hours planting, pruning, nurturing, discovering, budding, and blooming. We will chose to ignore or take the time to fully appreciate this single flower, just as we do this moment in Creation we call our life. We see the divine beauty and value or we just allow the flower and our days to proceed unnoticed and unappreciated until the bloom withers and the remains fall to the ground, an unexamined existence, just a series of events.

Trusting Ourselves/Embracing Our Divinity

Increasing our spiritual depth is sometimes difficult because we don't know where to start. Some decide, for instance to treat all life as sacred—seemingly a fairly clear and simple approach to guiding one's behavior: No alcohol. No smoking. No red meat. No abortions. No euthanasia. No cloning. No exceptions. Wouldn't it be nice if being more spiritual were as simple as following some rules? But even if we should happen to feel rewarded only by eating grains and fruits the rest of our life, we still have to decide whether to accept fish and dairy products and the effects of microwaves and the kind of fertilizers used. Should we destroy the habitat of the elephant or the spotted owl so we can have housing and croplands for humans and money to provide for their families? Is downsizing someone from their job and endangering their family's well being acceptable, so the company will do better financially and be rewarding for other families? Should we kill people who have killed other people so our communal existence is safer and less filled with fear?

We don't have to exercise our God-given opportunity to make tough decisions and to shape our lives and our world. But if we don't, someone else will shape it. We can live a life without particular reason, direction or purpose. Or we can demonstrate the fullness of our capabilities. It is our opportunity, our fate, our responsibility to co-create with God on this Earth. Since we are all equally supported children of the universe, why bother to act loving and caring? Why do good things? Why stand up against what is bad? Why not grab all we can, take what we want any way we can? It is because in our decisions we declare not only why we are here but also the nature of God. By our single life we have added a brush stroke to the picture of human existence and create not only our self-portrait but also the portrait of God on this planet. We have the opportunity as the highest form of Creation on Earth to actively bring a voice and consciousness to God. Do we have the courage to embrace our divinity and God's possibility?

> We are sinners, not because we do this or leave that undone, but because we refuse to follow our hopes, trust our desires, and obey our visions…preferring to unlive our lives because living them involves too much risk. (Werner and Lotte Pelz: God is No More.)

Erik Erikson was one of the earliest developers of the psychoanalytic notion that humans go through stages of personal and social development throughout our lives. He described the challenge of becoming a mature adult as resting on the struggle to find our own identity, to find our own self, accept it, and embrace it. We can never feel loved and give love freely, until we know who we really are and embrace our own identity. Until we honestly look at and fully accept ourselves with all our strengths and faults, we cannot fully offer ourselves in a relationship to someone else. Until then we have only presented a mask, an act we created in response to what others said we should be. Even when people act as though they like us, we can't feel loved if we haven't let them see who we really are. To enter into close, stable relationships, we must first know and accept the truth about who and how we are. We have to grow from structuring our lives to avoid our doubt, failure, fear, and guilt (or the lack thereof), to trusting that we are worthwhile even with our imperfections and mistakes—just like we are. We must accept the responsibility of making our own decisions and commitments, willing to risk disappointment or disapproval for the joy and fullness of living our own values, seeking our own revelations, and following our own vision.

On a moral, spiritual, and ethical level, the challenge is the same: to move from ideas and decisions based just on guilt, rules, and fear of punishment and alienation, to ideas and actions based on love, commitment, and responsibility. If we negotiate these succeeding stages of psycho-social and moral development, we never fear death because we have fully lived life. Erikson called this final challenge

Integrity vs. Despair. (Erik Erikson. Insight and Responsibility.) When we come to the end of our life, will we say:

I wish I could have done it differently.
or
I embrace all of it exactly like it was.

It is both liberating and frightening to realize we can live any way we choose. We have already fulfilled the need of the Universe just by perpetuating existence. Any additional purpose to our existence is left up to our own co-creation, the most amazing and awe-inspiring gift of being alive. Even the re-creation of human life no longer needs to be left to chance, love, or sex and no longer needs either mother nor father to bring it into existence. But out of all the possible human beings, we are the ones who are here. We are the voice God on Earth. Because of our choices and those of our ancestors and descendants, and a few million unforeseen events, our world continues to evolve in its unique and special way. Other forms and possibilities do not happen here. The genetic probability that you have dark or light skin, hair and eyes was pretty high. In fact we can clone an exact duplication, but the experiences we have, the decisions we make and the lives we lead, even if clones, will always define the meaning of our life and our individual uniqueness. The universe alters infinitesimally ahead in the direction we set. It is never going to be what it would have been without us, and is forever changed by our having been. What will we do with this opportunity? What is the legacy we will leave?

This choice about how we live is precisely what lifts our humanity above mere existence. The choices we make about how we live are our means to personal salvation. (Salvation: the state of transcending meaningless existence.) We are given a sliver of the history of time to live. It is our wonderful, special opportunity. We have more choice than any other species on our planet. Our power to express the nature of God is at the same time both minuscule and overwhelming, almost insignificant and infinitely important. The opportunity of our having come into existence is to take that which came from everything and make it into something more, to take that which is specially valuable and multiply its worth. Will we embrace our own divinity?

> My hands are small, I know.
> They're not yours.
> They are my own....
> God's hands.
> God's arms.
> God's eyes.
>
> (Hands. By Jewel Kilcher and Patrick Leonard. Recorded by Jewel.)

About The Author

Dr. Robert Blake combines theological and philosophical training from divinity school with thirty years experience as a clinical psychologist. He founded one of the first hospital based holistic health centers in the United States that integrated the treatment of mind, body, and spirit with both traditional and non-traditional medical approaches. He has taught at the university level as well as at local hospitals and churches. Currently he is doing what he loves best: maintaining a practice as a clinical psychologist and being part of the leadership team of a non-traditional church. His background in philosophy, theology, and medical psychology combined with both humorous story telling and a hard nosed scientist's quest for truth give him a unique background with which to offer a new understanding of spirituality and mankind's place in the universe.

Printed in the United States
941500004B